COMPETING IN THE NEW ECONOMY

Competing in the New Economy

Economy

Governance Strategies for the
Digital Age

Thomas W. Bonnett

Copyright © 2000 by Thomas W. Bonnett.

Library of Congress Number: 00-191777
ISBN #: Hardcover 0-7388-3264-2
Softcover 0-7388-3265-0

All rights reserved. No part of this book may be reproduced or transmitted in any form or by any means, electronic or mechanical, including photocopying, recording, or by any information storage and retrieval system, without permission in writing from the copyright owner.

Portions of this work were first published in *Is the New Global Economy Leaving the State-Local Tax Structure Behind?* (1998) and *Governance in the Digital Age* (1999) by the National League of Cities; and in *State Strategies for the New Economy* (2000) by the National Governors' Association. Used by permission.

Graphic on cover and in text used by permission. Economic and Social Impacts of Electronic Commerce. Copyright OECD, 1998.

Cover photo courtesy of the Kansas League of Municipalities.

Cover design by Kori Klyman.

This book was printed in the United States of America.
To order additional copies of this book, contact:
Xlibris Corporation
1-888-7-XLIBRIS
www.Xlibris.com
Orders@Xlibris.com

Contents

PREFACE
9
AN OVERVIEW
13
UNDERSTANDING THE NEW ECONOMY
21
GLOBALIZATION AND THE NEW ECONOMY
30
INFORMATION TECHNOLOGIES AND THE NEW ECONOMY
39
KNOWLEDGE—THE MOST IMPORTANT FACTOR OF PRODUCTION IN THE NEW ECONOMY
57
GOVERNANCE STRATEGIES FOR COMPETING IN THE NEW ECONOMY
69
ADAPTING TO CHANGE TO ENHANCE FUTURE PROSPERITY
127
ENDNOTES
133
APPENDIX A
157
APPENDIX B
161
SELECTED BIBLIOGRAPHY
175

RELATED WORK
    BY THE AUTHOR
    183
ABOUT THE AUTHOR
    185
ACKNOWLEDGMENTS
    187

Text Boxes, Tables, and Graphs

THE THIRD WAVE OF ECONOMIC GLOBALIZATION	31
INFORMATION TECHNOLOGIES INTEGRATE THE GLOBAL ECONOMY	33
THE GROWTH OF TRANSNATIONAL FIRMS	37
THE DIFFUSION OF TECHNOLOGICAL INNOVATIONS IS ACCELERATING	41
GROWTH IN INTERNET HOST COMPUTERS AND MAJOR E-COMMERCE DEVELOPMENTS	43
ECONOMIC DEVELOPMENT LESSONS FROM THE FIRST DECADE OF THE WEB	44
MEGAMERGERS IN 1998	45
COMPETITION ON A LEVEL PLAYING FIELD	46
TOP 25 U.S. COMPANIES	48
WILL THE INTERNET ENABLE PERFECT COMPETITION?	52
E-COMMERCE IMPACT ON VARIOUS DISTRIBUTION COSTS	54
RIDING THE STORM	55
THE OLD ECONOMY VS. THE NEW ECONOMY	59
KNOWLEDGE AS A KEY FACTOR OF PRODUCTION	62
WETWARE IN THE KNOWLEDGE ECONOMY	63
PATH DEPENDENCY AND THE NEW ECONOMY	65
DIGITAL LAWS DRIVING INTERNET BUSINESS MODELS	66
COMPARING THE OLD AND NEW ECONOMIES	68
REASONS TO ENHANCE THE VALUE OF PLACE	72
TRANSFORMING HOW WORK IS ORGANIZED	74
STATE GOVERNMENT AS A LEGACY SYSTEM	76

WHAT MIGHT 21ST CENTURY DIGITAL GOVERNMENT LOOK LIKE?	79
PROMOTING DIGITAL GOVERNMENT	81
THE PRIVATIZATION CONTROVERSY	84
MEASURING INPUTS AND OUTCOMES	86
ORGANIZATIONAL MODELS FOR THE 21ST CENTURY	90
THE ART OF PUBLIC MANAGEMENT	93
STRATEGIES TO TRANSFORM THE WORK OF STATE AND LOCAL GOVERNMENT	94
THE CHANGING NEEDS OF CHILDREN	98
STRATEGIES TO PROMOTE LIFE-LONG LEARNING	103
SOCIAL BENEFITS FROM PUBLIC R & D INVESTMENTS	109
TO CREATE AN INTELLECTUAL ENVIRONMENT	110
BUILDING COMPETITIVE ADVANTAGE	115
CLUSTERS AND THE NEW ECONOMICS OF COMPETITION	117
GLOBALIZATION COMPLICATES TAXATION OF CAPITAL AND INCOME	120
NGA POLICY ON EXPANDED DUTY TO COLLECT AND SIMPLIFICATION OF STATE SALES-USE TAXES1	123
STRATEGIES TO CREATE A HOSPITABLE ENVIRONMENT FOR THE 21ST CENTURY ECONOMY	126
THE NEW ROLE OF GOVERNMENT	130

PREFACE

I did not plan to write this book. No one asked me to write it or suggested it to me. Nor, did I sit at my desk one morning and think: "Hm, maybe I should write this book." Rather, the opportunity presented itself in this way.

In June of 1997, the National Governors' Association, the National Conference of State Legislatures, and the National League of Cities asked me to write a paper examining whether social and economic trends were threatening the viability of the traditional state-local tax structure. The product of that effort, *Is the New Global Economy Leaving the State-Local Tax Structure Behind?* was published in 1998.

Later that year, a group of seven national organizations serving state and local officials—the three above plus the Council of State Governments, International City/County Management Association, National Association of Counties, and U.S. Conference of Mayors—asked me to write a paper on the impact of the global economy, information technology and economic deregulation on state and local government. The result—*Governance in the Digital Age*—was published in June 1999 and has since won an Award of Publications Excellence. Both monographs were published by the National League of Cities and have been well received by the members of the sponsoring organizations. Indeed, I was asked during 1999 to make more than twenty presentations on these themes to public sector leaders throughout the country.

Also in the summer of 1999, Raymond Scheppach, the Executive Director of the National Governors' Association, asked me to write a paper about the New Economy. Portions of my work were included in NGA's Issue Brief: *State Strategies for the New Economy*, published for the winter governors' meeting in February 2000. Both NLC and NGA have graciously granted permission to use previously published material in this book.

A central theme of my work during the past three years is that state and local governments are behind in the race to enter the digital age. This book was written to focus immediate attention on three questions. What is this New Economy? What does it mean for the leaders of our state and local governments? What should community leaders do to compete in this New Economy?

Tons of business books have been published in recent years to explain the Internet, e-commerce, and how to use information technologies to transform business functions. There is no shortage of technical information about these topics either. We now have to work harder than ever before to screen out the noise—a mixed blessing of this information age—to prevent information overload from becoming oppressive. Yet, ironically, not much has been written for state and local officials, community leaders, and informed readers concerned about contemporary public policy choices stemming from the rapid advance of information technologies. I wrote this book to fill that void. I would be most pleased if some readers found value in this effort.

Thomas W. Bonnett
TWBPARKSLO@aol.com

COMPETING IN THE NEW ECONOMY:

Governance Strategies for the Digital Age

AN OVERVIEW

The phrase "*New Economy*" is on the fast-track to becoming an overused cliche. This is regrettable. A common response is to ask "What is so New about the New Economy?" Any dynamic economy adapts to changing social needs, consumer preferences, and new technologies. Responding to external forces, firms change how they organize work. "What makes this new economy so different from the old one?" ask the earnest skeptics.

The most frequent answers are abstractions. They cast gray shadows: the digital revolution, the Internet, the information age, globalization, high performance organizations, the changing nature of work, and so on. Each is only one thread of this new cloth.

The defining characteristic of this New Economy is that knowledge has become the most important factor of production. It is knowledge, after all, that enables individuals to create the new, new thing. It is the knowledge in organizations that enable them to exploit the new technologies to improve products and processes. The best technology on the planet sits on a shelf gathering dust unless someone is gifted enough to learn how to use it, and use it well.

Information technologies, artfully used by knowledge workers, have transformed the traditional manufacturing industries, are transforming the retail sector, and will soon transform much of the service sector as well. The digital revolution is richly celebrated, as it deserves to be, but it does not fuel itself. Knowledge fuels the digital revolution, which transforms industries and creates new forms of social wealth.

In the old economy, the source of wealth was in the land and its various riches. According to Lester Thurow, an MIT economist, the richest nations in the 19th century were those with the most valuable land, minerals, and natural resources. The industrial revolution begun in that century elevated the role of capital as a factor of production, but land remained a primary source of wealth throughout the world well into the 20th century. Thurow notes that ten of the twelve largest companies in the U.S. on January 1, 1900 were natural resource companies: American Cotton Oil Company, American Steel, American Sugar Refining Company, Continental Tobacco, Federal Steel, General Electric, National Lead, Pacific Mail, People's Gas, Tennessee Coal and Iron, U.S. Leather, and U.S. Rubber. Only one company, General Electric, survived the century in the top ranks.

In the old economy, our national comparative advantage was the ability to grow crops, to harvest natural resources, to mine the earth's bounty, and to produce tangible products to serve the social needs of a hungry nation. Those functions were the primary sources of wealth one hundred years ago. They remain important today, but the new sources of wealth are in what Thurow calls "brainpower industries."

At the beginning of 2000, General Electric was the second most valuable company in the U.S.—behind Microsoft. The stock market then valued Microsoft at more than a half a trillion dollars. Its book value (meaning what it would cost to replace its physical assets—its campus, buildings, and furnishings) was roughly ten billion dollars. Consider the variables that explain this gap in assessing the value of the company—its leadership, intellectual property, organizational capacity, the collective knowledge of its workers, relationships with suppliers, reputation with consumers, and its control of PC operating systems. *The most formidable of these corporate assets are intangibles.* Microsoft is the quintessential knowledge company. It spends $3 billion each year on research and development to try to stay ahead of the pack. And, it locks in the best talent it can find with stock options. (Not to be outdone, Intel has a venture capital portfolio of $4.8 billion.)

Don Tapscott, a business writer, is astute:

> Twenty-five years ago, Microsoft had no capital. Today Microsoft is the most valuable corporation in America, with a market capitalization now exceeding GE's. Twenty-five years from now, Microsoft may have no capital, if it loses its capacity to innovate.

Knowledge as A Factor of Production

Whereas at one time the decisive factor of production was land and later capital...today the decisive factor is increasingly man himself, that is, his knowledge.
Pope John Paul II, 1991

The new source of wealth is not material, it is information, knowledge applied to work to create value.
Walter Wriston, former Citibank president and CEO

The basic economic resource— the means of production, to use the economist's term— is no longer capital, nor natural resources (the economist's land), nor labor. It is and will be knowledge....Value is now created by productivity and innovation, both applications of knowledge to work.
Peter Drucker, 1993

Intellectual capital is intellectual material— knowledge, information, intellectual property, experience— that can be put to use to create wealth.
Thomas Stewart, 1997

The central event of twentieth century is the overthrow of matter. In technology, economics, and the politics of nations, wealth in the form of physical resources is steadily declining in value and significance. The powers of the mind are everywhere ascendant over the brute force of things.
George Gilder, 1989

The neo-classical economic theory identifies three factors of production: capital, labor, and land. In an industrial economy, wealth is created by adding more of these inputs to the production process, or improving the quality of how these inputs are used. The first is subject to diminishing returns, and the second is called technical progress.

The new growth theory puts human imagination and innovation at the core of the New Economy. Paul Romer, a Stanford economist, describes the economy as a well-stocked kitchen. What it lacks is a brilliant chef capable of using old ingredients to create new recipes. Here is Romer's metaphor, as described by Michael Lewis in his book about Silicon Valley:

> Only a very few people who wander into the kitchen find entirely new ways to combine old ingredients into delightfully tasty recipes. These people were the wealth creators. Their recipes *were* wealth. Electricity. The transistor. The microprocessor. The personal computer. The Internet.

America's comparative advantage was once its vast quantities of capital, labor and land (i.e., natural resources)—the traditional factors of production in the industrial era. In the emerging New Economy, America's competitive advantages are in the information technologies (the convergence of computing and telecommunications); its openness to foreign competitors, new products and services; its social flexibility to allow the shift in employment from "brawn to brains;" and its culture that celebrates and rewards those willing to innovate, creating new forms of social wealth.

A defining characteristic of this New Economy is the ability to innovate, the embrace of opportunities that result from change, the quest for the better mouse trap. The speed of innovation is another important trait. Entrepreneurs building Internet businesses equate a Web year with a dog year (one seventh of a human year). The pace of economic activity has been accelerated by the advances in information technologies, especially the Internet.

Jack Welch of General Electric calls the Internet "the single most important event in the U.S. economy since the Industrial Revolution." The protocol for the World Wide Web was developed in Switzerland in 1989—hardly more than a decade ago. Of the estimated 171 million users of the Internet in 1999, roughly half lived in the U.S. and Canada. In stark contrast, half of the world's population has never touched a telephone. America's ability to adapt to change is a distinct competitive advantage in this global marketplace.

In physics, when acceleration accelerates, it is called jerk. The New Economy is jerking us into a frantic pace of innovation, change, new products, new services, new firms, and new business models. This wave of advanced information technologies, the knowledge workers who create and exploit these technologies, and the genius of organizers to provide a nurturing environment for them are the three pillars that define this New Economy. This has important implications for state and local economic development strategies, and for all of government as well. The public sector needs to learn how to do the business of government better, faster, cheaper.

Competing in the New Knowledge Economy

Strategies to compete in the 21st century economy flow from our understanding how the digital revolution and the integrated global economy are eroding the traditional advantages of geography. Roughly 85 percent of the goods and services we consume daily are produced within our national borders. That will change. The world is shrinking, metaphorically, as transportation and telecommunications systems become more advanced and cheaper. The digital convergence of computing and communications partly overcomes the tyranny of geography. The Internet has accelerated the rapid diffusion of information. Capital mobility has become instantaneous.

The forces of the digital revolution and global competition transcend geographic boundaries. The link between work and geography is unraveling. The economic production of many goods and services is being uncoupled from consumption. What does this mean for our states and cities, which are bounded by lines on a map?

Elected officials should to ask themselves this question: *"If work is portable, and knowledge workers can choose where they live, then why might these knowledge-intensive firms and their workers choose to locate and live in my community?"* The best answers to this question include these phrases: *"enviable quality of life... outstanding public services, especially schools, health care, transportation and airports...career opportunities... job mobility...hospitable and supportive environment for entrepreneurs..."*

Reasons to Enhance the Value of Place

Regional and national economies are becoming integrated into the global economy. Both international trade and direct foreign investment are growing at a faster rate than world output.

Capital and other factor of production are becoming very mobile. Walter Wriston, former Citibank CEO, has noted, "MONEY GOES WHERE IT IS WANTED AND STAYS WHERE IT IS WELL-TREATED."

The digital revolution will enable a growing share of knowledge work to be performed anywhere in the world. Peter Drucker notes, "KNOWLEDGE KNOWS NO BOUNDARIES."

The trend of decreasing place-based investments by the federal government will continue to increase the burden on the state and local governments to ensure the economic viability of their communities.

Source: Bonnett, GOVERNANCE IN THE DIGITAL AGE (Washington, D.C.: National League of Cities, 1999), 15.

The firms with the greatest mobility in the future will rate the quality—specifically the quality of life in a community—as more important than the cost of its location. To a greater extent than in the past, these firms will locate where they can attract the best talent, and these knowledge workers will be able to afford to live where they wish. To compete in the 21st century economy, the public sector leaders must invest strategically to enhance the value of place, which means high quality public services and institutions, mobile and accessible transportation systems, safe and secure communities, and a healthy physical environment.

States and cities need 21st century strategies to enhance the value of place as the forces of the digital revolution and the integrated global economy transcend geographic boundaries. They need new approaches to promote life-long learning because knowledge has become the dominant factor of production in this new economy, the skills required for jobs in the 21st century economy will be steadily rising, and job churning will be even higher than it is today. Strategic public investment in physical infrastructure is necessary to improve the quality of life in our communities.

State and local governments must learn from leading service sector firms about benchmarking, performance-based measures and accountability, and how to best use purchasing, privatization, and markets to achieve social outcomes. Public sector organizations must adapt quickly and effectively to respond to changing social needs.

Governors and mayors need to engage the public in establishing social priorities and in the process of experimenting with new approaches to achieve them. Citizens will require both "high tech and high touch" services. The state and city governments also need a fresh approach to economic development that eases burdens on small businesses, assists entrepreneurs, cultivates venture capital formation, and rewards innovation.

Competing in the New Knowledge Economy will require all this and more. This book explains why. It also explains how state and local governance strategies can improve the economic viability of our communities in the midst of turbulent social and economic changes.

Understanding the New Economy

The phrase "New Economy" is winning the popularity contest over its rivals: the Digital Economy, the Internet Economy (or, its shorter version, the Net Economy), the Information Economy, and the Network Economy. Yet, as it gains in popularity among journalists, the phrase is losing its saliency. We frequently hear news reports that label the surging Nasdaq as the New Economy, and the declining Dow Jones industrial average as the Old Economy. Here, by comparison, is a range of conceptual interpretations of the term:

♦ To those involved in information technologies (i.e., computing and communications), the New Economy is a short-hand description of the power of these new communications tools to create new products and companies with lightning speed, establish relationships with consumers that eliminate the intermediaries (e.g., the wholesalers and distributors), and transform how business can be done in the digital age.

♦ To a venture capitalist, the term represents hundreds of opportunities each day to invest in new startup firms that could create new products and services, leap into the equity markets, and create untold private wealth for both entrepreneurs and investors.

♦ To a corporate leader, the New Economy means forming new alliances, partnerships, or mergers to form powerful organizations to enter new markets, achieve greater efficiencies, and gain market share.

- To a trade advocate, the term is often linked to the benefits from expanding international trade, growing direct foreign investment, and lower national tariffs—which together accelerate the trend toward creating an integrated global economy.

- To an educator, the New Economy means the children today must surpass yesterday's skill levels in math, computing, language, and science to be prepared for the jobs of the 21st century. It also means the public sector must invest more resources to promote early childhood education and experiment with new ways to extend life-long learning opportunities for adults.

- To the average citizen, the New Economy signifies a range of digital opportunities at home, including to shop online; find work or new employment; obtain hobby-related information; conduct business, travel planning, electronic banking, day trading in the stock market; and pursue a host of activities (computing, entertainment, and communications) via the Internet.

- To some intellectual critics, the New Economy represents the latest chapter in a decades-old saga about the drift of sovereignty from democratically elected national and state governments toward markets (and those who are active in them). To others, the New Economy is a fundamental shift of power from all traditional institutions in society (government, academia, the media, religion, and others) to individual citizens as they gain more information, choices, and personal autonomy.[1]

The implications of this New Economy to governors, mayors, and community leaders should be apparent. The twin forces of globalization and the digital revolution are eroding the traditional advantages of geography. Political jurisdictions, however, are bounded by lines on the map. If production becomes uncoupled from consumption, the states and cities must invest strategically to enhance the value of place to compete for mobile firms and the knowledge workers. Life-long learning becomes a major theme for new governance strategies to expand learning opportunities for all citizens because knowledge has become the dominant factor of production, the skill levels for the jobs of the future are rising, and job churning is increasing.

Public sector managers must look to innovative firms in the service sector for lessons on how to transform the business of government, by using information technologies, by establishing performance-based accountability, by privatization, and by respecting the power of markets to achieve social outcomes. Lastly, economic development officials must redesign their programs to reduce regulatory burdens on small business, assist entrepreneurs, cultivate venture capital formation, form public-private partnership, and make better use of the intellectual capital of the state universities to improve the ability of regional and local economies to adapt to accelerating social change.

This book will develop these ideas further, but first this discussion requires greater clarity of some basic concepts. When a phrase like the New Economy is widely used, it often becomes a cliche, losing its explanatory value. It is necessary to filter through the clutter resulting from its overuse to clarify this term, beginning with its adjective.

"What's So New About the New Economy?"

This seminal question was first posed by Alan Webber, a former editor of the *Harvard Business Review*.[2] Market economies are always changing, always shifting, always responding to internal and external forces. Personal tastes change, social needs also change. New products are introduced. New firms are formed. Firms that fail to adapt to changing demands lose market share, and some die. Of the 25 biggest firms in 1960, only 6 remained on that list in 1997.[3] New technologies and new markets emerge, providing entrepreneurs with new opportunities. The new competes against the old. Competition in the market economy, to use Joseph Schumpeter's memorable phrase, is a "perennial gale of creative destruction."[4] In this context, what distinguishes this New Economy from the inherent "creative destruction" of a market economy?

According to Anthony Carnevale, a labor economist, writing in 1991:

> In the old economy competitive success was based almost exclusively on the ability to improve productivity. In the new economy organizations and nations compete not only on their ability to improve productivity but on their ability to deliver quality, variety, customization, convenience, and timeliness as well.

Carnevale emphasizes the role for a more highly skilled workforce in the New Economy:

> Workers' skills need to be both broader and deeper especially at the point of production, service delivery, and at the interface with the customer in order to meet new competitive standards and to complement flexible organizational structures and technology.[5]

Alan Webber answered his own question by linking the knowledge of both workers and managers to use technologies wisely with the traditional virtues of trust and communication:

> The move to a new economy takes managers on a journey. It's a voyage that begins with technology and leads inexorably to trust....The revolution in information and communications technology makes knowledge the new competitive resource. But knowledge flows through the

technology: it actually resides in people—in knowledge workers and the organizations they inhabit. In the new economy, then, the manager's job is to create an environment that allows knowledge workers to learn—from their own experience, from each other, and from customers, suppliers, and business partners.[6]

We Americans have a love for technology, and for good reasons too. (One scholar uses the word, *Neuerungsfreundigkeit*, to describe "the love of new things which is a crucial mark of Western culture."[7]) We live, sings Paul Simon, " in a time of miracle and wonder." Arthur C. Clarke, the visionary (space satellites) and author (*2001 Space Odyssey*), once wrote "any sufficiently advanced technology is indistinguishable from magic."

The digital convergence of all forms of communication—voice, data, text, video, audio—is profoundly reshaping our economic and social institutions. This digital revolution is transforming both the function and form of modern organizations, as well as shifting more information and autonomy to individuals. It is driving the domestic economy and accelerating the pace of change. Just within the past year, a growing number of respected economists have joined the chorus of technology cheerleaders in heralding the *Digital Economy* as the defining characteristic of this transitional path from the old industrial era to the New Economy of the 21st century.[8]

Alan Greenspan, Chairperson of the Federal Reserve Board, has testified in Congress that this wave of information technology has stimulated economic growth, led to productivity gains, and eased inflationary pressures during the longest peacetime expansion in this century.[9] John Cassidy, a financial journalist, presents supporting views from Greenspan's colleagues:

> "We are really undergoing a revolution in technology," Robert D. McTeer, Jr., the president of the Dallas Fed told me.

"The technology is pushing economic growth forward and making productivity grow faster. As the same time, globalization has increased competition and removed firms' pricing power, which restrains inflation." Edward G. Boehne, the president of the Philadelphia Fed, agreed with McTeer. "We may very well be in a period that is comparable to what people were going through a century or so ago with the Industrial Revolution, except this time around it is the computer and telecommunications," he said. "You never really know for sure while you're in it, but it increasingly looks like we are in one of those technological leaps forward."[10]

It would be difficult to overstate the potential significance of information technologies (the merger of computing and communications) on the domestic or global economy in the coming decade and beyond.[11] But technology, by itself, is never a panacea, nor is it omnipotent. The value of technology must be understood in a social context. As Webber observed, technology is but a tool. Its wise use requires knowledge. The best new technology, sitting on the shelf, has no inherent value to others unless they have the skills and knowledge to use it well, in ways that improve business processes and make them more efficient, more productive.

This reasoning is why a younger generation of economists are investigating the creation of social wealth in this information age by looking at technologies as the tools, knowledge workers as those capable of using them well, and the social environment which enables both to flourish. Is there something special about the social context in which technology is allowed to blossom? When is it easily adapted to improve operations? How does it shape new entrepreneurial ventures? How well do organizations adapt to changing markets and external forces? What is the social context that enables organizations to exploit the power of new technologies and employ the knowledge of their human resources to create social value? On a practical level, are there lessons to be learned from the leading firms in the service sector about how to transform the nature of work? Lessons that elected officials and managers in state and local government might value?

Market economies place strong pressure on firms to adapt to change. The relative openness of the American economy is one of our national competitive advantages. "Why have not the same available technologies allowed productivity in Europe and Japan to catch up to U.S. levels?" asked Greenspan. A short version of his answer: American firms experience relentless pressure to restructure work, making best use of the skills of workers and new technology.

Greenspan's longer response emphasized the American flexibility of both labor and capital markets, less onerous government regulations, fewer trade restrictions, and more flexible systems of corporate governance compared to those in Europe and Japan. In Austria, someone who wants to open a drug store must first gain the approval of all pharmacists. Similarly, Japan protects traditional retailing by restricting department stores. Japan is also most creative in using non-tariff barriers to prevent foreign imports from competing against their domestic goods and services. Its trade officials once claimed that American-made skis could not be sold in Japan because its snow was different.[12]

America has the largest, most affluent market in the world. Its demanding consumers drive producers to meet their high expectations. Its remarkable openness to new goods and services allows new firms to challenge old ones. Its labor and capital mobility allow both to flow to more productive uses. These economic and social dynamics drive change, and reward those who successfully respond by innovating, creating, and adapting. Economists adore efficiency so they embrace organizational flexibility and labor mobility. Others see this phenomenon differently because job churning is increasing. Job churning results from job creation from new firms and job loss from business failures. This is why new initiatives to enhance skills have become a top priority of our governments at all levels.

Essential to this New Economy are the entrepreneurs, who are creative and willing to take risks, and innovative managers willing to adapt to changing markets, new technologies, and new knowledge. Douglass C. North, an economic historian, puts great emphasis on the concept of "adaptive efficiency", which he defines as "the kinds of rules that shape the way an economy evolves through time." North continues:

> It is also concerned with the willingness of a society to acquire knowledge and learning, to induce innovation, to undertake risk and creative activity of all sorts, as well as to resolve problems and bottlenecks of the society through time.[13]

The New Economy is defined as the emergence of knowledge as a factor of production, the ability of both entrepreneurs and organizational leaders to develop and exploit new technologies, and the social environment that nurtures and stimulates innovation. These themes are implicit in this description of the emergence of the knowledge-based economy:

> During the past five years there has been a unique combination of focused market incentives that have led to immense technical progress in the areas of computing, biotechnology, telecommunications, and transportation (to name only a few) and which have begun to foster dramatic changes in the way in which economies, organizations, and governments will function in the future. Indeed, *there is compelling evidence that the sudden and ever-accelerating burst of growth in high-technology and high-skill services and in the new products and service structure they are creating may bring about some of the most profound and unexpected changes to the way in which we live and work witnessed since the nineteenth*

century transition from an agricultural to an industrial society.[14] (Emphasis added.)

The New Economy can be viewed through three powerful lenses: globalization, information technologies (IT), and the concept that knowledge has become an important factor of production. The first two are external, driving forces of change. The third lense emphasizes the social ability to respond to these external forces in new ways that create social wealth. A brief discussion of each topic provides direction to elected officials and community leaders seeking to redesign state and local governments. New governance strategies are needed to ensure that our communities remain economically viable and prosperous in the digital age that lies ahead.

GLOBALIZATION AND THE NEW ECONOMY

Globalization, a truly ugly word, means the liberalization of the movement of goods, services, capital, and people throughout the world. It is not a new phenomenon. One could say that it stretches back for 500 years, since Christopher Columbus acted on the wild idea of sailing west to pursue the riches of India. The pace of globalization has varied, of course. The movement of people across national borders was less constrained by governments in the 19th century than during most of the 20th century. Thomas Friedman, a foreign columnist for the *New York Times*, has noted that except in times of war, most immigrants traveled without a national visa or passport prior to 1914.[15] Indeed, the first two-thirds of our national history was distinguished by having remarkably open borders, which allowed millions of immigrants to flow into this land of freedom and opportunity. Rigid immigration quotes were not established as national policy until the 1920s.

Friedman also notes that the current level of trade in goods as percent of world output is comparable to international trade in the early part of the 20th century. This historical parallel has led some economists to understate the significance of the current phase of globalization as a force in accelerating change in the U.S. economy.[16]

Ernest Preeg, a trade expert, has defined three distinct phases of globalization in the 20th century, and concludes that the current wave has unleashed a tremendous force that is changing the modern economy. Preeg identifies three characteristics of the current phase of globalization:

The Triumph of Economic Liberalism;
The Information Technology Revolution; and
The Internationalization of Private Sector Enterprise.

The Third Wave of Economic Globalization

1. *The Triumph of Economic Liberalism.* National markets opened dramatically to increased competition, internally and externally, throughout the 1980s and into the 1990s. The United States took the lead in broadscale deregulation, followed by the United Kingdom and, more recently, other industrialized countries. Trade liberalization...continues...in order to achieve full international "contestability" of national markets....

2. *The Information Technology Revolution.* The rate of technological change, based on the rapid development of information-based technologies, is truly revolutionary in impact by any historical standard....Its impact, now pervasive and of growing consequence in virtually all sectors of the economy— manufacturing, agriculture, telecommunications, financial services, transportation, medical services, and education— will increase further due to the recent advent of open internet communications....

3. *The Internationalization of Private Sector Enterprise....*The international exchange of goods, services, capital, technology, management skills, and labor are all expanding. The leading-edge sectors that are both cause and effect of the globalization process are those which constitute the new infrastructure for trade--financial services, telecommunications, and transportation....One consequence of this internationalization is a strong trend toward vertical integration of production across borders by MNCs [multinational corporations]....

This third wave of globalization, moreover, is different and more far-reaching, in function and geographic terms, than anything that has gone before.

Source: Preeg, *From Here to Free Trade*, 4-5.

Dismantling the Berlin Wall in 1989, a symbol for Preeg's first argument, marked the beginning of the 21st century. Since that historic event and the subsequent unraveling of the former Soviet Union in 1991, the leaders of most nations have embraced markets as the engine of economic progress. In *The Commanding Heights*, Daniel Yergin and Joseph Stanislaw cite the many national leaders who have rejected the seductive idea that "command and control" by their governments could accelerate the growth of their economies. Deng Xiaoping, after a life time of devotion to the Communist Party, demonstrated surprising pragmatism upon assuming leadership in China in 1978. He said, "It doesn't matter whether a cat is black or white as long as it catches mice." Deng also defended his efforts to encourage private investment: "I have two choices. I can distribute poverty or I can distribute wealth."[17]

The story of how information technology has integrated regional and national economies into the global realm is best told by Walter Wriston, the former president and CEO of Citibank. In his 1992 book, Wriston tells of how international telephone circuits between Brazil and New York were so rare in the 1950s that dialers were employed—"squads of Brazilian youth who did nothing but dial phones all day long"—and who would stay on the line, once obtained, "reading newspapers or books, filibustering to keep the line open until someone actually needed it." Contrast Wriston's anecdote with the estimated hourly average of 100 million telephone calls, using some 300 million access lines, that were completed worldwide in the 1990s.[18] Indeed, two economic historians have noted:

> The best transatlantic telephone cable in 1966 would carry only 138 conversations between Europe and North America simultaneously. The first fiber-optic cables, using lasers for transmission, were installed in 1988 and had the capacity to carry 40,000 conversations simultaneously. The fiber-optic cables installed in the early 1990s have an even greater capacity.[19]

The recent development of the Internet as a new communications medium has overshadowed the long-standing advances in telecommunications and transportation. A three-minute telephone call between London and New York City cost $244 in 1930; while air travel per passenger mile in that year cost $0.68. In 1990, the same 3-minute transatlantic phone call cost $3.32 while air travel cost just $0.11 per passenger mile (in constant dollars).[20] Another scholar estimates the cost of the U.S. to London telephone call declined by 90 percent from 1987 to 1997.[21]

> ## Information Technologies Integrate the Global Economy
>
> Information and communications technologies have allowed us to create an instant world that recognizes no limits to geography, time or information-processing, communications or decision-making capacities, ore economic or political boundaries for that matter. And it is they more than any other single factor that are facilitating the integration of world commerce, exposing national markets, industries, and companies to competition and introducing great instabilities in international financial markets....Estimates are that over one trillion dollars in foreign currencies were trading hands in these electronic markets in 1993 by traders, speculators, and institutional investors all over the world. The speed and volumes of these flows already threatens the financial stability of the world economy and they are continuing to grow.
>
> Source: Maurice Estabrooks, *Electronic Technology, Corporate Strategy, and World Transformation* (Westport, CT: Quorum Books, 1995), 3.

These telecommunications advances have combined with equally impressive gains in computing to form a digital convergence of information technologies. *Capital has always been the most mobile factor of production, but now it has wings.* Electronic networks, using secure cables, between banks and governments have enabled tremendous volumes of transactions to flow throughout the world rapidly, if not instantaneously. The international foreign exchange settlement system transfers an estimated $1.25 trillion each day.[22] In addition, the Federal Reserve's Fedwire and the New York-based CHIPS facilitate the transfer of more than 2 trillion dollars each day. Adding the several billions of dollars flowing through the credit and debit card systems to that estimate led one scholar to conclude: "The combined dollar flow in one day equals over one-third of our gross domestic product for the entire year."[23]

The production of standardized goods had been shifting to developing nations over several decades. General Electric makes light bulbs in Korea, Reebok makes sneakers in Thailand, AT&T makes telephones in Indonesia, Spaulding makes soccer balls in Pakistan, and Levi Straus has announced it will soon end its domestic production of blue jeans, and so on.

The digital convergence of information technologies and telecommunications—the most distinguishing characteristic of this wave of globalization—has enabled transnational corporations to decentralize and disperse core production and design functions of high-value added products throughout the world. The Boeing 777 jet plane is built from components manufactured in twelve different countries. Robert Reich presents this example of modern global production networking:

> Precision ice hockey equipment is designed in Sweden, financed in Canada, and assembled in Cleveland and Denmark for distribution in North America and Europe, respectively, out of alloys whose molecular structure was researched and patented in Delaware and fabricated in Japan. An advertising campaign is conceived in Britain; film footage for it is shot in Canada, dubbed in Britain, and edited in New York.[24]

For centuries, trade volumes—the value of domestic exports and foreign imports—were the major indicator of how much a national economy was integrated with another nation or the world economy. In the current phase of globalization, capital is extremely mobile and production is becoming more mobile than ever before. Economists who focus on trade volumes, today, are viewing the trees, not the forest. Boris Pleskovic of the World Bank makes this sobering comparison, "In Ricardo's day, the value of traditional merchandise trade dwarfed financial flows. In 1998, global merchandise exports totaled $5.2 trillion for the year, a value that financial flows reached on an average day."[25]

The mobility of capital and production notwithstanding, we may well have good reasons to be optimistic about the future because the American economy has distinct competitive advantages in this global economy. However, we have no reasons to be complacent because the forces driving globalization also have the power to neutralize our national advantages. To cite an obvious example, research laboratories are frequently attached to production facilities, and the combination frequently leads to the new wave of innovation. Locations hosting research laboratories and state-of-the-art production facilities may possess first-mover competitive advantages in the next production cycle.[26]

Like capital, knowledge—the core of the New Economy—is also mobile. Bangalore, India is one of the fastest growing concentration of computer programmers in the world. A business consultant makes this telling observation:

> This electronic corporate globalization is already occurring. More than 100 American firms, for example, outsource their software "code cutting" to sites in India, where the work is completed and returned overnight electronically by highly skilled programmers at only a fraction of the labor costs demanded in the U.S. In fact, it is estimated

that as many as 4 million "virtual aliens" are employed directly in the American workforce—residing outside the nation's borders, undercutting traditional labor markets, paying no taxes—connected only through electronic telecommunications networks.[27]

Telecommunications transcends distance and information technologies flatten organizational structures. Taken together, this digital revolution has facilitated a wave of transnational mergers and acquisitions. Daimier-Benz acquires Chrylser, Berttelsmann buys Random House, Amoco takes over British Petroleum, Deutsche Bank tries to buy Bankers Trust, Ford wants to buy Volvo and so on. This wave of global organization—to maximize scale and scope, to rationalize operations, to enter new and emerging markets—has been a prominent trend since the 1960s. There is little doubt, however, that the profound advances in computing and communications in the past decade have increased the ability of managers in these transnational firms to direct larger organizations. The digital revolution is facilitating a global management revolution.

So, *"its a small world after all."* The world is shrinking, metaphorically, as transportation and telecommunications systems become more advanced, cheaper, and more reliable. Capital mobility has become instantaneous. The digital convergence of computing and communications has partly overcome the tyranny of geography, flattened organizational structures, and facilitated economic aggregation. The organization of transnational firms both reflects and advances the trend toward an integrated global economy. The latter have become prominent advocates for international trade agreements that harmonize the business environment across national boundaries.[28] Today, the Internet holds tremendous potential to improve communications and facilitate electronic commerce around the globe.

> ### The Growth of Transnational Firms
>
> Worldwide, over the past decade, foreign direct investment has been growing four times faster than world trade. In 1995, multinationals invested $325 billion overseas. The fact that roughly a third of trade flows are payments within individual companies shows that most companies have production systems stretching around the world. According to the United Nations, there are close to 40,000 "transnational" companies, three times the figure 25 years ago. Together they control about a third of all private-sector assets, and their combined GDP in 1993 was $5.5 trillion— almost as much as that of the United States.
>
> **Source**: John Micklethwait and Adrian Wooldridge, *The Witch Doctors: Making Sense of the Management Gurus* (NY: Times Books, 1997), 228.

For these reasons, Preeg concludes that this third wave of globalization is far more significant than the previous two phases. The opening of national markets from economic deregulation and lower national tariffs forces domestic industry to become more competitive. The development of information technologies, such as computing and the Internet, transcend geographic boundaries, enabling electronic commerce to flourish without regard to location. The fastest growing economic sectors are stimulated by accelerating direct foreign investment, capital mobility, and other factors of production throughout the world. These aspects of globalization—accelerating the accelerated pace of change—led another author to call this phenomenon "*Turbo-capitalism.*"[29]

Elected state and local policy makers should understand how this current phase of globalization is stimulating the transition toward the New Economy. The major conclusion is simple: the American states and cities are not competing against one another for firms, knowledge workers, or the jobs of the future as much as they are competing against the rest of the world. Our jurisdictions will win relatively few jobs based on solely on low wages; the developing nations will win most of those. America's strongest competitors will be those nations (e.g., Japan and Europe) that have economies most similar to ours. Despite the substantial first-mover advantages we enjoy, the pace of global competition will force the state and local governments to organize the brainpower to capture the growth industries of this New Economy.

Lester Thurow, an MIT economist, makes this point eloquently:

> The most rapidly growing industries in the 1990s and the early part of the twenty-first century: microelectronics, biotechnology, the new material science industries, telecommunications, civilian aircraft manufacturing, machine tools and robots, and computers (hardware and software)...are manmade brainpower industries that could be located anywhere on the face of the earth. Where they will be located depends upon who organizes the brainpower to capture them.[30]

States and cities have long assisted firms to promote their exports in international markets and have recruited direct foreign investment in their economies. They are appropriate economic development activities, but fall woefully short of promoting wealth creation in the New Economy. The leaders in state and local government must take bold action to invest in public infrastructure, revise their government operations, and develop new strategic approaches to economic development to compete in this global economy. Those strategies will be discussed in the second half of this book, but first the driving force of information technologies in this New Economy must be explored in greater detail.

Information Technologies and the New Economy

For those of us who once thought the IBM Selectric was a nifty typewriter, we are simultaneously amazed at the advances in computing and overwhelmed by the incessant rhetoric of industry cheerleaders about the social transformation and the digital revolution. Some dismiss the latter hyperbole outright, others respond with cynicism. Dave Barry, one of our finest humorists, notes, "The Internet is the most important single development in the history of human communications since the invention of 'call waiting.'"[31] On the other hand, *"Jack Welch of General Electric, one of those people who created conventional business wisdom every time he opened his mouth, said that the Internet was 'the single most important event in the U.S. economy since the Industrial Revolution."*[32]

Public sector leaders can inhabit the comfort zone between the cynics and the cheerleaders, but they need to understand why Welch made his assessment. From day to day, we are unlikely to perceive the profound impact the digital revolution is having on economic and social relationships, but the underlying trend is significant. For example, this country had approximately 5000 computer programmers in 1960; now we have 1.3 million. Today, a Ford Taurus or Palm Pilot has more computing power than the Apollo 11 did in 1969, taking Neil Armstrong to the moon and back. The average American household now has more computing power than existed in the world in 1965. The price of microprocessors continues to decline steadily as they grow more powerful and faster. According to Moore's law, the power of microprocessors doubles every 18 months—a trend that has constant since Moore, a cofounder of Intel, first made this observation in 1965.[33]

Information technologies are clearly driving the domestic economy today. According to a Department of Commerce study, "Between 1995 and 1998, these IT-producers...contributed on average 35 percent of the nation's real economic growth." (Information technologies can be defined by 3 Cs: *Computing, Communications,* and the *Convergence of digital technologies* in these two industries.) The Commerce report also estimated: "By 2006, almost half of the U.S. workforce will be employed by industries that are either major producers or intensive users of information technology products and services."[34]

Information technology (IT) is an essential element in this New Economy. First, IT is accelerating the rate of economic change, which is creating boundless opportunity for entrepreneurs. Second, IT is facilitating the changing the form and function of business organizations in the modern economy. Third, IT has the potential to restructure state and local government services and operations. Elected officials and public sector managers should understand these three potential impacts of information technology to help them revise economic development strategies to enhance the value of place in the digital future.

Most are familiar with the story of the development of the Internet. During the 1960s, the Department of Defense provided funding to teams of university researchers to develop computer networks to share data with each other. The precursor to the Internet was formed when common protocols were developed that allowed university computers to transfer files and, later on, electronic mail. In 1982 only a few hundred university computers were part of this ARPAnet. Throughout that decade, the National Science Foundation provided additional funding for a parallel system, which expanded the number of university computers using this packet-switched protocol to transfer files and communicate with each other.

In 1989, Tim Berners-Lee, working at a high-energy physics lab in Switzerland, developed a protocol called the World Wide Web. This, the now ubiquitous WWW, used hypertext to link together different documents on the Internet. The singular act of genius by Berners-Lee was quickly followed by a collective act of inspiration and creativity. In 1993, a team at the University of Illinois developed the first version of Mosaic, " a tool that provided a unified interface for several different protocols used on the Internet," according to Hal Varian, a business professor at the University of California. Varian continues, "Mosaic's graphic support...added a whole new dimension to exploration of the Internet....pictures add the 'gee whiz' factor that made people excited about the Web."[35]

The Diffusion of Technological Innovations Is Accelerating

The Internet's pace of adoption eclipses all other technologies that preceded it. Radio was in existence thirty-eight years before fifty million people turned in; TV took thirteen years to reach that benchmark. Sixteen years after the first PC kit came out, fifty million people were using one. Once it was opened to the general public, the Internet crossed that line in four years.

Source: *The Emerging Digital Economy*, U.S. Department of Commerce, April 1998, 4.

This story reveals more about the entrepreneurial culture of Silicon Valley than a dozen books. Berners-Lee, ever the serious researcher, thought adding images to the Mosaic browser was frivolous ("This was supposed to be a serious medium; this is serious information," he lectured Marc Andreessen.) Yet Jim Clark, the founder of Silicon

Graphics, was looking for an new venture. He recruited Andreesen without a clear idea of what kind of business to pursue. Together, they traveled back to the Illinois campus and successfully recruited most of original Mosaic team to join this startup enterprise. Initially called Mosaic Communications, the startup firm became Netscape. Its major product became the most popular software ever developed commercially (mostly because Netscape made its browser available to so many for free). In August 1995, sixteen months after Netscape was formed, it entered the public equity market and was valued at $2 billion on the first day of its Initial Public Offering (IPO).[36]

Michael Lewis reports this IPO may have been the most famous of all time—the IPO heard round the world. It attracted such attention that a flood of capital soon began to flow into new ventures that promised to transform how business could be conducted. John Doerr, a high-profile venture capitalist in Silicon Valley, proclaimed that what happened in the late 1990s was "the greatest legal creation of wealth in the history of the planet."[37]

Prior to the development of Mosaic, the WWW protocol accounted for less than one percent of the Internet backbone's traffic—indeed, it was ranked the 127th largest source of traffic among the many Internet protocols. The graphics component, of which Andreesen was proud, was exploited brilliantly first by the Mosaic team and then by Netscape and others. Within a few short years, the WWW exploded with growth and soon carried as much traffic as the other Internet protocols combined. From a handful of web pages in 1993, this medium grew to more than 50 million web pages by 1999.[38] A U.S. Department of Commerce report, *Digital Economy 2000*, claims there are "more than one billion web pages, with an estimated three million new pages added each day." A new medium of communications had evolved.

The graph below shows the exponential growth of the Internet since 1982 when a several hundred computers were linked together with common protocols (ARPAnet). Note this chart uses a log scale measure the growth (each increment on the vertical scale increases by the power of ten). The number of Internet host computers grew to more than 10 million in less than two decades. Also note the significant developments along this soaring path: the WWW protocol invented in 1989—just one decade ago; the decision of NSF to lift restrictions on commercial use of the Internet; the Mosaic browser invented at the University of Illinois in 1993; the rapid exploitation of this new application by Netscape in 1994 with its Navigator browser; and the creative genius of young companies such as Dell, Cisco, and Amazon to use the Internet for commercial transactions. This is this epochal story of the new economy shaping the digital age.

Growth in Internet host computers and major e-commerce developments

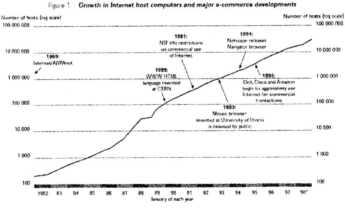

Source: *The Economic and Social Impacts of Electronic Commerce: Preliminary Findings and Research Agenda*, OECD, September 1998.

To appreciate the dramatic effects of this digital revolution, public sector leaders must understand how information technology is transforming how business is organizing its activities and how work itself is changing. Pushed by increased global competition, American-based corporations used information technologies in the 1980s and 1990s to reengineer business processes and reduce the number of full time employees. One in five U.S. workers was employed by a Fortune 500 company 25 years ago; now fewer than one in ten is.[39]

Economic Development Lessons from the First Decade of the Web

Governments should invest in basic science and research. The social benefits from the Internet are many times greater than the cost of federal support to computing and communications technologies. Unless intellectual property rights are fully secured, individual firms will never invest enough in research and development because they will be unable to capture the full stream of benefits. Government can make these investments, which benefit society. Prior to federal investment in research and development— stimulated by World War II— state-sponsored research at their universities was the prominent means of exploiting applied scientific developments to enhance regional economies.

Celebrate individual genius, but do not neglect the team. Hypertext was an old idea (from 1945), and Tim Berners-Lee was able to develop the WWW protocol to make it work. Mosaic was a team effort performed in a federally funded university project (National Center for Supercomputing Applications). Its development was not an assigned task. Furthermore, the team subsequently rebelled at the NCSA's rigid supervision.

Illinois lacked the entrepreneurial culture to transform the Mosaic browser into a commercial enterprise. Said Andreessen, "There is no infrastructure at all in Illinois for a startup company. It's not there. No one does it." Silicon Valley, flush with gifted engineers and venture capitalists, had the entrepreneurial culture to nurture Netscape. [As a bitter sweet side note, The University of Illinois sought compensation from Netscape, alleging its products were based on the initial Mosaic browser. The University declined an allotment of Netscape stock (which peaked at a value of $17 million) and took a cash settlement instead, estimated at $2 million.]

The first mover advantage of Netscape's browser was eroded after Microsoft incorporated its Explorer browser into its popular Windows 95 operating software, and also gave it away free. That triggered an antitrust suit against Microsoft by the U.S. Department of Justice, which has been appealed to the U.S. Supreme Court. In late 1998, Netscape was acquired by America Online in a stock swap valued at $4.2 billion.

IT facilitates the flow of information from the top and the bottom to each other; it enables organizations to eliminate the middle layers of managers, and decentralize decisions to those in the front lines. This trend, along with new organizing principles such as Just-In-Time inventory, explains why many business experts suggest that the old business model, the fully vertically integrated firm, is archaic in this new economy.[40] The Ford Motor Company once raised its own sheep for its car upholstery, until its management realized its expertise was not in sheep ranching.

The latest wave of information technology has had paradoxical effects on business organizations, what an economist might call "aggregation and disaggregation." Aggregation simply means that the big often get bigger. Note below the list of ten megamergers in 1998. According to one business writer, the top seven were the largest mergers of all time. The total value of merger activity was more than twice that of 1997, and greater as a percent of GNP than the first great U.S. merger wave 100 years ago.[41] Information technologies have enabled large corporations to become even larger. In 1999, mergers and acquisitions worldwide totaled an estimated $3.4 trillion. In the areas of financial services, telecommunications, energy, and automobile production, these corporate leaders have demonstrated their faith in seeking the scale and scope from building, in the words of one business expert, "multinational megacompanies."

Megamergers in 1998 (in Billions)

Exxon and Mobil ($86)
Travelers and Citibank ($73)
SBC Communications and Ameritech ($72)
Bell Atlantic and GTE ($71)
AT&T and Tele-Communications ($70)
Nationsbank and BankAmerica ($62)
British Petroleum and Amoco ($55)
Daimler-Benz and Chrysler ($40)
Norwest and Wells Fargo ($34)
Banc One and First Chicago ($30)

Source: Geoffrey Colvin, "The Year of the Megamerger," *Fortune*, January 11, 1999.

Remaining unanswered is the question of how well the scale and scope of such large corporations will fare against the speed and flexibility of the *gazelles*—David Birch's term for small, rapidly growing, often venture-backed companies that frequently capture new market opportunities before the corporate giants can complete their annual strategic planning processes. The amazing success of so many of these new companies, either as IT-producers or as innovative exploiters of IT, has prompted many business experts to celebrate this entrepreneurial wave as the *Digital Economy*, the *Network Economy*, and the *Internet Economy*. As examples, one thinks of Amazon, Yahoo!, eBay, Cisco, Dell, Gateway, and, of course, Microsoft.

Competition on a Level Playing Field

Time and distance will no longer be a factor in decision making. Information will be available simultaneously, globally....

The Internet levels the playing field between countries, between states and between companies regardless of size, in a way that has never occurred before. Even in the industrial revolution, you had to have large amounts of capital to be competitive. In today's revolution, all you need is a Web site. Set up the right way, with the right idea, you can suddenly compete with the biggest companies in a way that was never possible before. It doesn't mean that the big companies won't win. But it does mean that there is a level playing field between them.

Source: John Chambers (CEO of Cisco Systems), "Preparing for the New Economy," Special Issue, *Government Technology*, August 1999, 18.

Mary Meeker, an investment banker with Morgan Stanley Dean Witter, has been very critical of the giant media companies for not exploiting the potential of the Internet. Says Meeker, "Disney should have been Yahoo, AT&T should have been A.O.L., Time Warner should have been Excite. Why didn't it happen? It was a series of judgment errors."[42]

According the Thurow, ten of the top twelve companies in this country at the beginning of the 20th century were natural resources companies. They included the American Cotton Oil Company, American Steel, American Sugar Refining Company, Continental Tobacco, Federal Steel, National Lead, Pacific Mail, People's Gas, Tennessee Coal and Iron, and U.S. Leather. One hundred years ago, we had a natural resource economy.[43] That was the old economy, based on processing raw materials into standard products for mass consumption.

The only company remaining on the top twelve list of U.S. companies is General Electric. Significantly, GE has recently been pushed out of the top spot by Microsoft—the quintessential knowledge-based firm in this digital era. Don Tapscott, a leading business writer, notes:

> Twenty-five years ago, Microsoft had no capital. Today Microsoft is the most valuable corporation in America, with a market capitalization now exceeding GE's. Twenty-five years from now, Microsoft may have no capital, if it loses its capacity to innovate.[44]

Below is a list of the top 25 U.S. companies based on market capitalization as of December 31, 1999. More than half of these firms were not on this list twenty years ago. Two of the newcomers resulted from megamergers (Citigroup and Exxon Mobil) and two are giant retailers (Wal-Mart and Home Depot). But most of the newcomers, the ones highlighted in the accompanying textbox, are dominant in the information technology industries of communications, computing, and convergence—in short, the IT firms driving the U.S. economy. Most of these IT powerhouses had not even been started in 1979. Even Wal-Mart owes much of its success in the past decade to its sophisticated use of Just-In-Time inventory data—an application of IT—so that store managers can stock what the customers want to buy.[45]

> **Top 25 U.S. Companies**
> (In millions, market capitalization on Dec. 31, 1999)
> *Microsoft* ($602,432)
> General Electric ($507,216)
> *Cisco* ($366,498)
> Wal-Mart ($307,865)
> *Intel* ($275,007)
> *Lucent Technologies* ($235,117)
> Exxon Mobil ($195,588)
> IBM ($194,455)
> Citigroup ($187,500)
> *AOL* ($169,617)
> American Intl Group ($167,403)
> *SBC Communications* ($165,523)
> AT&T ($162,365)
> *Oracle* ($160,187)
> Home Depot ($158,234)
> Merck ($157,053)
> *Yahoo!* ($152,600)
> *MCI WorldCom* ($151,190)
> Procter & Gamble ($144,152)
> Coca-Cola ($143,876)
> Johnson & Johnson ($143,131)
> *Dell Computer* ($130,823)
> Bristol Myers Squibb ($127,359)
> Pfizer ($125,574)
> *Sun Microsystems* ($120,966)
>
> Source: *Wall Street Journal*, February 24, 2000, R13

The recent flood of investor dollars into emerging Internet companies follows a well-established pattern. Investors frequently demonstrate a strong appetite for bold, new technologies that hold the potential of transforming society. The reason for this is obvious: A $100 investment in Intel in its initial public offering in 1972 was worth $162,338 in December 1998.

Stock market bubbles were common in England and the U.S. in the 19th century following the development of railroads and the telegraph. During the roaring 1920s, investors were very enthusiastic about the automobile and electric industries, and especially the new medium for mass communications—the radio.[46] The 1998–99 Internet stock bubble is no exception to that pattern. According to one industry index, the Internet stock bubble leaked about thirty percent, in terms of market value, from its peak in April to August 1999. Market values rose again, reaching 4000 on the Nasdaq composite index by January 2000, peaked at 5048 in March, then slid to 3164 in late May, but returned to above 4000 by late June—almost regaining its January level.[47]

The most significant observation about this flood of capital into Internet-related firms, however, came from Bill Gates, whose personal net worth topped $100 billion in 1999. When he was asked about the market boom in stock values of Internet companies—a trend that Alan Greenspan equated to buying a lottery ticket—Gates said the analysts have missed the most important point. Gates responded, in the reporter's words, *"Whether or not it's a bubble, it is attracting enormous amounts of capital to every imaginable Internet-related company, and this influx of cash is going to drive 'the pace of Internet innovation even faster.'"*[48]

The paradox of aggregation and disaggregation occurring simultaneously requires a dip into economic theory. Ronald Coase wrote a short essay in 1937 in which he posed an important question: "If production is regulated by price movements...why is there any organization?" In effect, Coase was asking: if markets are so wonderful, why do we organize economic activity through firms. The abbreviated answer is that hiring full time workers and owning business equipment enables the managers to reduce the transaction costs of contracting with others to execute the firm's core production functions. Understanding the concept of *transaction costs* is key to understanding how information technologies alter organizations. Coase observed, "Changes like the telephone and the telegraph which tend to reduce the costs of organizing spatially will tend to increase the size of the firm. All changes which improve managerial technique will tend to increase the size of the firm."[49] Professor Coase won the Nobel prize for Economics in 1991.

Information technologies—computing, communications, and the digital convergence of both—facilitates the transmission of quick, cheap information throughout any organization. It reduces transaction costs. It enables organizations to decentralize its operations, to reduce hierarchies, to empty warehouses by using Just-In-Time inventories, to contract with multiple suppliers, to sell the sheep ranch and buy wool in competitive auctions from multiple bidders. It enables organizations to become larger or smaller—by removing barriers to entry. *The size of the firm will be less significant to its competitive prospects in the future than in the industrial era: what matters most today is the firm's ability to innovate, use new technologies and the knowledge of its workers to seize new market opportunities, and anticipate how to exploit its core competencies in rapidly changing business environment.*

The painful lesson that command and control in business hierarchy was failing in the competitive market was first learned by U.S. manufacturing firms in the 1970s and 1980s when they were losing market share to foreign imports. These firms implemented quality reforms, began reengineering efforts, adopted JIT methods to reduce inventories and shift responsibilities to suppliers, and adopted high-performance organizational approaches such as using teams and decentralizing authority to the front lines. A similar revolution is taking place now in retailing as electronic commerce competes with "bricks and mortar" stores. The top managers in state and local government need to learn from the business innovations developed by leading firms in the service sector, many of which can be applied to improve public sector operations.

By threatening existing patterns and relationships, the digital revolution provides tremendous opportunities to new ventures and new ways of conducting business. Home Depot has reduced its need for intermediate warehousing—85 percent of its merchandise comes directly to its retail stores from manufacturers. According to one case study, "sales associates walk through the aisles, electronically recording orders for products that need to be restocked; orders are sent for fulfillment over the Internet..."[50] According to another business expert, 245,000 businesses in this country provide intermediary services—think of brokers, commercial agents, wholesalers. In a world of perfect information, their services are vulnerable. Stock brokers are threatened by E-Trade, Ameritrade, and others. Will the traditional "bricks and mortar" retail stores on Main Street or in the shopping malls be threatened by online retail shopping? According to the Garner Group, economic forecasters:

> The Internet retail market will grow from $16 billion in 1999 to $142 billion in 2004, a compound annual growth rate of 53 percent. Analysts expect entertainment and essential home consumables (such as food) will experience significant gains, reaching $26 billion and $6 billion, respectively, during the same five-year period. Banking and financial revenues for brokerage and online banking will reach $12 billion by 2004.[51]

When business writers use a phrase such as "the Internet business model" or the dreadful word, *disintermediation*, they are referring to the potential of information technologies to transform how business can be conducted—directly threatening existing firms and traditional business patterns. Once again, Bill Gates provides a key insight:

> As the interactive network assumes the role of market maker in category after category of goods and services, traditional middlemen will have to contribute real value

to a transaction to justify their commissions. *Stores and services that until now have profited just because they are "there—in a particular location, for example—may find that just being there is no longer enough.* But the middlemen who provide added value will not only survive, they will thrive, because the information highway will let them make their services available to customers everywhere. (Emphasis added)[52]

Will the Internet Enable Perfect Competition?

There are no barriers to entry, no protection from failure for unprofitable firms, and everyone (consumers and producers) has easy and free access to all information. These just happen to be the three main characteristics of Internet commerce...The Internet lowers the cost of comparison shopping to zero. Increasingly, the consumer can easily and quickly find the lowest price for any good or service. In the cybereconomy, the low-cost producer will offer the lowest price and provide this information at no cost to any and all potential customers anywhere on the planet.

Edward Yardeni, chief economist for Deutsche Bank, as quoted by Friedman, *The Lexus and the Olive Tree*, 66-7.

Anecdotal evidence is mounting daily in support of Gates' proposition that the digital revolution will facilitate "friction-free capitalism." An estimated 39 percent of American adults had access to the Internet at home or at work in 1999. "Nearly Half of U.S. Homes Now Have Access to Web," reports the *Wall Street Journal* in June 2000.[53] Dell Computer reports its online sales doubled in 1998 and reached a daily average of $18 million in the first quarter of 1999, or 30 percent of its $5.5 billion first quarter revenues. Dell estimates online sales will grow to produce half of its revenues in 2000.[54] Staples began its online sales on November 11, 1998; a year later, Staples.com reported $200 million in first-year revenues. Thirty percent of individual stock trades in 1999 were being conducted electronically. The *Wall Street Journal* reports a new anxiety in the corporate world: "Those who hesitate risk being *amazoned*, forfeiting business to an Internet newcomer, in the way that bookstore chains have lost ground to Amazon.com Inc., the online bookseller."[55] Gates has also been quoted as predicting that one-third of all grocery shopping will be done electronically by 2005.

Not every expert agrees with Gates, however. Michael Dertouzos, Director of the MIT Laboratory for Computer Science, thinks that electronic commerce may never overcome the trust barrier, except for commodity items. For that reason, Professor Dertouzos thinks no more than fifteen percent of all daily commerce will ever be conducted electronically.[56] This important issue of trust explains why Charles Schwab has been so successful integrating its electronic trading with its traditional services in branch offices to form the new business model for retail—"clicks and mortar."[57] Business analysts at IBM, though, estimate that at much as one-third of the $8 trillion national economy could be conducted electronically within the coming decade.

Coase's notion of transaction costs is evident in the chart below, which assesses the E-commerce impact on various distribution costs. The traditional system means physical transactions. A person goes to the neighborhood travel agent to buy an airline ticket. This costs the agent $8 per transaction, while an electronic airline ticket costs the provider only $1.00 per transaction. Similarly, a person making a banking transaction in a branch facility with the assistance of a teller imposes a cost of $1.08 on the bank. The same transaction conducted via the telephone costs the bank only half as much—$0.54. PC banking, however, only costs the bank $0.13; it saves the bank 89 percent of its costs compared to that of operating, staffing, heating, lighting, and securing a branch bank facility. Industry experts contend that electronic banking via the Internet would cost the bank just one cent. Any industry subject to robust competition will move toward the most efficient means of conducting its core business. James

Culberson, President of the American Bankers' Association, anticipates that half of all banking transactions will be conducted electronically and one-third of bank branches will close in the future.

E-commerce impact on various distribution costs

($US per transaction)

	Airline Tickets	Banking	Bill Payment	Term Life Insurance	Software Distribution
Traditional System	$8	$1.08	$2.22-$3.32	$400-$700	$15
Telephone-Based		$0.54			$5
Internet-based	$1	$0.13	$0.65-$1.10	$200-$350	$0.20-$0.50
Savings (percent)	87%	89%	67-71%	50%	97-99%

Source: *The Economic and Social Impacts of Electronic Commerce: Preliminary Findings and Research Agenda*, OECD, September 1998, 30.

The debate on how quickly electronic commerce will grow misses the most important point—change is inevitable. The important question for public sector leaders is: How does the public sector benefit from this tidal wave toward electronic commerce? In the spring of 1999, Forrester Research predicted business-to-business e-commerce will rise to $1.3 trillion in 2003; within days, the folks at Intel said that estimate was too low. In June 2000, Jupiter Communications estimated that business-to-business electronic commerce in the U.S. "is expected to grow to $6 trillion by 2005 from $336 million now."[58]

Firms, new or old, that exploit the potential of digital commerce to compete vigorously will thrive; those that do not will fail. GE bought more than $1 billion worth of goods and services via the Internet in 1997," and claims it will save $500–700 million by making $5 billion in purchases of goods and services via the Internet over the next three years.[59] According to the OECD study, "Cisco first allowed customers to purchase equipment over its Web site in 1996 and generated $100 million in sales; sales reached over $1 billion in 1997 and are expected to reach $4 billion in 1998."

> ### Riding the Storm
>
> Some months ago, Lou Gerstner, the boss of IBM, dismissively described the thousands of new "dot.com" companies springing up as "fireflies before the storm." The storm would arrive, he said, when the really big firms— the Global 1,000— seized the power of the Internet and used it to transform themselves. This week saw almost simultaneously announcements...from the world's two biggest car makers, to say that they are moving their entire supply chains on to the Internet. Mr. Gerstner's storm has arrived with hurricane force.
>
> On November 2nd first Ford and then General Motors declared that their huge purchasing operations would swiftly transfer to the web, connecting suppliers, business partners and customers from all over the world by means of giant online markets....Both firms are showing how big companies in a range of industries are likely to use the Internet to put themselves at the centre of new e-business ecosystems that will transform their entire way of doing business.
>
> **Source:** *THE ECONOMIST*, November 6, 1999, 63.

The application of IT to transform business activities, which is accelerating the rate of change, has been the glitter that has enticed millions of investors (and scores of witless day traders) to buy Internet lottery tickets. It also explains why traditional state economic development strategies are missing the mark: the New Economy requires a changing role for the public sector to facilitate the creation of wealth in a digital, knowledge-based society.

Of the estimated 171 million users of the Internet in 1999, roughly half lived in the U.S. and Canada. In stark contrast, half of the world's population has never touched a telephone. That competitive advantage, as with most first-mover advantages, will not last for long without prudent support by the public sector. How the states and cities can embrace this digital revolution to enhance the value of their communities in the global economy is addressed in the following chapters.

KNOWLEDGE— THE MOST IMPORTANT FACTOR OF PRODUCTION IN THE NEW ECONOMY

In his book, *The Lexus and the Olive Tree*, Thomas Friedman makes a forceful argument that once technology had enabled change, but now it is driving change.[60] The rapid pace of change, new products, new companies, and new technologies makes the contemporary period seem special, perhaps unique. And, in many ways, it is. Yet, an OECD study notes that the current era is not the first time "that our societies have been exposed to the broad diffusion of information and communications technologies." The report observes, "Over the 20-year period from 1874 to 1895, the typewriter, telephone, phonograph, electric light, punch card, hydro-electric plant, automated switchboard, cinema and radio were all invented."[61]

The sociological question, asks Robert Pool, a science writer, is "If technology shapes society, what shapes technology?" Pool contends that the causality pushes in both directions: society shapes technology just as technology shapes society. A related question concerns the timing and necessary social conditions to support a new technology: when and how does technology become adopted throughout the society.[62] According to Brian Winston, a communications scholar, the facsimile prototype was patented in 1843. And Winston notes, "The idea of television was patented in 1884. Digitization was demonstrated in 1938. Even the concept of the 'web' dates back to 1945." And yet, the development of these technologies for widespread use came many, many decades later and required special circumstances.[63]

These qualifications are important because we often attribute too much credit to technology for personal and social progress. Inadvertently, we undervalue the ability of people to make these tools work well and the flexibility of organizations to make artful use of both to create social value. The New Economy is not limited to high-tech industries. Every sector of the U.S. economy becomes more efficient, productive, and competitive when new technology is employed and people are able to "apply knowledge to knowledge," in Peter Drucker's memorable phrase, to improve business operations.

Notice how much technology and knowledge have in common. Both are essential to compete in this New Economy. Both require supportive social environments to flourish. Both often have a short shelf life—they may become obsolete quickly so they require constant maintenance and reinvestment. Both are difficult to value as personal or organizational investments because the future earnings on these investments are impossible to predict, which leads many to under invest in them. The power of each is magnified by the combination with the other one. The firms most likely to succeed in this New Economy understand the value of employing new tools and the best talent and skills of their employees. Public sector leaders must understand this as well. State and local governments are in the service sector. Applying knowledge to work is essential in managing public resources, organizing service delivery, and making strategic investments to improve the quality of life in our communities.

The story of Boeing's development of its 777 jet illustrates how organizations must be flexible to incorporate new technologies in this New Economy, which puts a premium value on knowledge workers to use them well. This plane was designed using computer-assisted design (CAD), unlike past aircraft designed and built from blueprints. The design team included personnel from various airlines throughout the world committed to purchasing the plane. In other words, the customers were given opportunities to design the product to better meet their needs. Boeing claims the team approach and the

CAD process saved the company as much as twenty percent of its $4 to $5 billion development cost.[64] This approach also may have given Boeing a competitive edge against its rival Airbus Industrie of Europe in the market segment for large transoceanic airlines.[65]

The Old Economy Vs. the New Economy

The Old Way
Build an airplane and deliver it.
Make paper drawings and full-scale mockups.
Test fly to discover blunders.
Separate all work functions.
Write maintenance manuals last.

The New Way
Customer participates in design.
Paperless, no mockups.
Computer simulation removes bugs.
Design-build teams.
Mechanics involved throughout.

Source: Don Tapscott, *The Digital Economy*, 144.

Each 777 airplane includes 1300 microprocessors, which prompted Don Tapscott, a savvy business strategist, to ask: "What does it mean to be a "manufacturing" company in the new economy?" His answer, "One-third of the cost of a Boeing 777 is software. So Boeing is clearly in the software business, and the new value leader in creating aircraft might be a company with leading-edge software development capabilities, such as Microsoft, EDS, Andersen Consulting, or IBM."[66]

Economists since David Hume and Adam Smith have understood that knowledge has an essential role in most economic activities. Because it was so difficult to quantify, knowledge was not part of the neo-classical economic model, which emphasized three factors of production in the wealth creation process: capital, labor, and land (i.e., natural resources). Indeed, land was the primary source of personal and national wealth for most of human civilization. Then in the 19th century, when capital fueled the industrial revolution, it began to rival land as the dominant factor of production. Only in the middle of the 20th century did skilled labor, as it became one of our national comparative advantages, rise in importance as a factor of production. Lester Thurow observes, "Natural resource endowments have fallen out of the competitive equation....After correcting for general inflation, natural resource prices have fallen almost 60 percent from the mid-1970s to the mid-1990s."[67]

The neo-classical model, and the economic development strategies drawn from it, still fit the industrial era when the primary economic output was tangible goods—cars, refrigerators, toasters, and shower curtains. During this period, state and local governments sought to improve the quantity of these primary factors of production to promote economic development. Increasing inputs is subject to diminishing marginal returns; improving how they are used is called technical progress.

Today, wealth is increasingly generated by the creation and application of knowledge. The post-industrial society, the digital economy, the information age, the knowledge economy—these phrases each reflect the economic transformation that emphasizes intellectual capital as the new factor of production. Peter Drucker offers this historical interpretation:

> Forty years ago, in the 1950s, people who engaged in work to make or to move things were still a majority in all developed countries. By 1990 they had shrunk to one-fifth of the workforce. By 2010 they will be no more than one-tenth. Increasingly the productivity of manual workers in manufacturing, in farming, in mining, in transportation can no longer by itself create wealth....From now on what matters is the productivity of non-manual workers. And that requires *applying knowledge to knowledge*.[68]

Employment growth for several decades has been in the service sector, especially in many new jobs requiring knowledge and advanced skills. One economist estimates that 63 percent of the jobs in this service sector are "considered to be in the high-skill categories."[69] According to the U.S. Labor Department, the domestic economy gained more than thirty million jobs from 1979 to 1998. Only 4.4 million of these jobs were in the least-skilled categories of blue collar and personal services. Most of the net job creation—18 million jobs—occurred in the categories that required advanced education or skills: professional, technical, or managerial positions. A Clinton administration report, *21st Century Skills for 21st Century Jobs*, notes that of the eight of the ten fastest growing jobs of the next decade will require college education or moderate to long-term training. Virginia Postrel, writing in the *Wall Street Journal*, explains that a majority of new jobs, as projected by the Bureau of Labor Statistics, will require both specific skills and the ability to employ knowledge:

> What all these jobs have in common, regardless of their educational requirements, are specific skills and a great deal of employee discretion. Many also reward the ability to interpret and respond to the unpredictable moods and actions of other people. In short, they all employ knowledge workers.[70]

Academic economists, seldom bounded by reality, produce theory that lags behind empirical trends. Until Robert Solow's 1958 seminal work on a growth model, most conventional economists accepted the neo-classical factors of production, and the law of diminishing marginal returns to scale. Growth, according to that model, came from increased inputs of capital, labor or land. Solow, however, concluded that only half of the U.S. growth could be explained by increasing inputs of capital or labor. Indeed, he estimated only 20 percent of the increase in GNP could be attributed to the stock of capital. (Many economists were displeased—they like to study what they can count.) An economic journalist explains:

> Something else was at work, because growth rates far exceeded what could be explained by the standard account. The growth attributable to some other inexplicable source Solow called the "Residual"....The consensus today is that Solow's famous Residual reflects the influence of technology

and industrial organization, factors not studied systematically by conservative economists.[71]

> **Knowledge as A Key Factor of Production**
>
> *Whereas at one time the decisive factor of production was land and later capital...today the decisive factor is increasingly man himself, that is, his knowledge.*
> — Pope John Paul II, 1991
>
> *The new source of wealth is not material, it is information, knowledge applied to work to create value.*
> — Walter Wriston, former Citibank president and CEO
>
> *The basic economic resource— the means of production, to use the economist's term— is no longer capital, nor natural resources (the economist's land), nor labor. It is and will be knowledge....Value is now created by productivity and innovation, both applications of knowledge to work.*
> — Peter Drucker, 1993
>
> *Intellectual capital is intellectual material— knowledge, information, intellectual property, experience— that can be put to use to create wealth.*
> — Thomas Stewart, 1997
>
> *The central event of twentieth century is the overthrow of matter. In technology, economics, and the politics of nations, wealth in the form of physical resources is steadily declining in value and significance. The powers of the mind are everywhere ascendant over the brute force of things.*
> — George Gilder, 1989

Solow's work was followed by Edward Denison's analysis of productivity in the domestic economy, which estimated that "the advance in managerial and organizational knowledge was a large source of growth in 1948–73."[72] A younger generation of economists, building upon the work of these giants, extended economic theory on growth in promising directions. These have included research on human investment, technological diffusion and economic growth; a new growth model that emphasizes endogenous technological change; and a growth model driven by the discovery of new ideas throughout the world (which benefits the U.S. because our economy is much more open than most others).[73]

Gary S. Becker, an economist who received the Nobel prize for this work on human capital, explains this concept: "Wealth in the form of human capital consists of present and future earnings because of education, training, knowledge, skills, and health." Furthermore, Becker notes, "Human capital is estimated to be three to four times the value of stocks, bonds, housing, and other assets."[74] A major responsibility of governments has been to make social investments, especially through public education and health, to enhance human potential and expand economic opportunity.

Wetware in the Knowledge Economy

We will take our imagery and language from the ongoing digital revolution and refer to these three different types of inputs as hardware, software, and wetware. Hardware includes all the nonhuman objects used in production--both capital goods such as equipment and structures and natural resources such as land and raw materials. Wetware, the things that are stored in the "wet" computer of the human brain, includes both the human capital that mainstream economists have studied and the tacit knowledge the evolutionary theorists, cognitive scientists, and philosophers have emphasized. By contrast, software represents knowledge or information that can be stored in a form that exists outside of the brain. Whether it is text on paper, data on a computer disk, images on film, drawings on a blueprint, music on tape-yen thoughts expressed in human speech--software has the unique feature that it can be copied, communicated, and reused.

Source: Richard R. Nelson and Paul M. Romer, "Science, economic growth and public policy, *Challenge*, March 13, 1996.

The twin pillars of this New Economy are information and knowledge. They are fundamentally different from the traditional factors of production. Knowledge is nonrivalrous (which means it can shared with others often without diminishing its inherent value to its creator); and, in Thomas Jefferson's phrase, knowledge is "infinitely expansible."[75] Or, consider Kal Seinfeld's advice to his son, Jerry: "You can only make a certain amount with your hands, but with your mind, it's unlimited."[76]

Paul Romer, a Stanford economist, describes the modern economy as a well-stocked kitchen. What it lacks is a brilliant chef capable of using old ingredients to create new recipes. Here is Romer's metaphor, as described by Michael Lewis in his book about Silicon Valley:

> Only a very few people who wander into the kitchen find entirely new ways to combine old ingredients into delightfully tasty recipes. These people were the wealth creators. Their recipes *were* wealth. Electricity. The transistor. The microprocessor. The personal computer. The Internet.[77]

The work of W. Brian Arthur, another Stanford economist, also provides important insights to those seeking to understand the New Economy. Arthur's key concepts include positive feedbacks, increasing returns, path dependency, and market lock-in. Positive feedbacks create uncertainty in the market. Increasing returns means the swiftest often enjoy the spoils of victory, while the slower competitors fall further and further behind. Path dependency occurs when an innovation becomes so broadly accepted that it become the unofficial standard for that product. (QWERTY, the top row of the keyboard, is frequently used as an example of this. The letters were first organized more than a century ago so that typewriter keys would not stick, yet within a decade most manufacturers had adopted this design and most workers had learned this system: it remains the unofficial standard today.) Market lock-in, the fantasy of every red-blooded entrepreneur, is the outcome of these developments. Arthur explains:

> Increasing returns are...mechanisms of positive feedback that operate—within markets, businesses, and industries—to reinforce that which gains success or aggravate that which suffers loss. Increasing returns generate not equilibrium but instability: *If a product or a company or a technology—one of many competing in a market—gets ahead by chance or clever strategy, increasing returns can magnify this advantage, and the product or company or technology can go on to lock in the market.* More than causing products to become standards, increasing returns cause businesses to work differently, and they stand many of our notions of how business operates on their head.[78] (Emphasis added.)

Path Dependency and the New Economy

Because small, random events that happen early can be magnified to have great importance later, the eventual outcome can depend quite sensitively on circumstances— it is path dependent. A chance laboratory discovery may push a developing technology in an entirely different direction than it would have taken otherwise....A computer language developed for early computers, which had relatively little power or memory, becomes the standard that shapes the programs written for much more powerful computers a decade later. In particular, Arthur notes, such path dependency implies that the outcome cannot be predicted with any certainty ahead of time. When VCRs were first offered for sale, no one knew which format would predominate.

Source: Pool, *Beyond Engineering: How Society Shapes Technology*, 157.

The Old Economy was based on processing raw materials into consumer goods for the mass market. Natural resource development and industrial production were its core economic activities. The factors of production were ruled by the law of diminishing returns. The business model during the industrial era was the vertically integrated firm.

The New Economy is based on information and knowledge, the new factor of production. The new economic principles are increasing returns to scale and path dependency. Innovation and technical advances are understood by managers as strategic weapons that lie inside the business process. Each of these characteristics places a premium on organizations that are flexible, strategic, and lightning fast to create new products and services. Organizations must be able to exploit new technologies and unleash the talents and skills of their employees to succeed. The Internet is a disruptive technology.[79]

Digital Laws Driving Internet Business Models

Moore's Law: Computing power doubles every 18 months.

Metcalfe's Law: "The power of computers on a network rises with the square of the total power of computers attached to it. Every new computer both uses the Net as a resource and adds resources to the Net in a spiral of increasing value and choice."

Gilder's Law: The total bandwidth of communications systems will triple every 12 months in the coming decade.

Gates' Law: Cannibalize your own product to keep first-mover advantage.

Moore's law is generally understood by consumers as computing devices continue to gain power and speed at lower cost. In their seminal book, *Information Rules: A Strategic Guide to the Network Economy*, Carl Shapiro and Hal Varian, two Berkeley professors, write, "The information age is built on the economics of networks, not the economics of factories."[80] Metcalfe's law explains the concept of network effects: the value of joining a network increases exponentially as more people join it.[81] Or, conversely, as the vaudeville comedians in the 1920s used to ask, "Who was the idiot who bought the first telephone? There was no one to call."

Business writers often use the word *cannibalize* to describe how firms destroy their own product line as they introduce new waves of products employing the latest technologies. Don Tapscott writes that Microsoft's DOS was the best selling software of all time when Microsoft introduced its Windows 95 operating system.[82] Firms are still searching for the best business model in this New Economy, but it will not be the vertically integrated firm that characterized the old industrial economy.

A comparison of the Old and New Economies, published by the Progressive Policy Institute in July 1999, is presented below. This is an adaption of an earlier construct by John Doer of Kleiner, Perkins, Caulfield & Byers—one of the most successful venture capitalists in Silicon Valley. The value of these archetypes is the clear dichotomy framed between the Old and the New Economy. See also "10 Driving Principles of the New Economy," from *Business 2.0* (<www/business2.com/services/10principles.html>).

	Old Economy	New Economy
Economy-wide Characteristics:		
Markets	Stable	Dynamic
Scope of Competition	National	Global
Organizational Form	Hierarchical, Bureaucratic	Networked, Entrepreneurial
Potential Geographic Mobility of Business	Low	High
Competition Between Regions	Low	High
Industry:		
Organization of Production	Mass Production	Flexible Production
Key Factor of Production	Capital/Labor	Innovation/Knowledge
Key Technology Driver	Mechanization	Digitization
Source of Competitive Advantage	Lowering Cost Through Economies of Scale	Innovation, Quality, Time to Market, and Cost
Importance of Research/Innovation	Moderate	High
Relations with Other Firms	Go it Alone	Alliances and Collaboration
Workforce:		
Principal Policy Goal	Full Employment	Higher Wages and Incomes
Skills	Job-specific Skills	Broad Skills, Cross-Training
Requisite Education	A Skill	Lifelong Learning
Labor-Management	Adversarial	Collaborative
Nature of Employment	Stable	Marked by Risk and Opportunity
Government:		
Business-Government Relations	Impose Requirements	Assist Firms' Innovation and Growth
Regulation	Command and Control	Market Tools, Flexibility

Source: *State New Economic Index*, Progressive Policy Institute, Washington, D.C., July 1999, 5.

The public sector can learn how to organize work from the most innovative firms in the private sector. Their trials and turmoil over the last two decades provide valuable lessons to elected officials and public sector managers. Drawing from those lessons, the next chapter discusses governance strategies for the public sector to compete in this new economy.

Governance Strategies for Competing in the New Economy

Globalization and the digital revolution are powerful forces reshaping society and its organizations. The policy choices facing governors, county executives, and mayors today could not be more urgent. Public sector leaders who understand these external forces and act strategically to facilitate the New Economy will ensure that their communities continue to prosper in the 21st century.

Goal #1: To Enhance the Value of Place in the Digital Age

Strategies to compete in the 21st century economy flow from our understanding how the digital revolution and the integrated global economy are eroding the traditional advantages of geography. Roughly 85 percent of the goods and services we consume daily are produced within our national borders. That will change. The world is shrinking, metaphorically, as transportation and telecommunications systems become more advanced and cheaper. The digital convergence of computing and communications partly overcomes the tyranny of geography. The Internet has accelerated the rapid diffusion of information. Capital mobility has become instantaneous.

Francis Cairncross in her book, *The Death of Distance*, writes

"No longer will location be key to most business decisions. Companies will locate any screen-based activity anywhere on earth."[83] Michael Porter, in a recent *Harvard Business Review* article, presents this assessment:

> Now that companies can source capital, goods, information, and technology from around the world, often with a click of a mouse, much of the conventional wisdom about how companies and nations compete needs to be overhauled. In theory, more open global markets and faster communication should diminish the role of location in competition...[84]

Yet our political jurisdictions are bounded by lines on the map. The forces of the digital revolution and global competition transcend geographic boundaries. The link between work and geography is unraveling. The economic production of many goods and services is being uncoupled from consumption.

Public sector leaders should ask themselves this question: *"If work is portable, and knowledge workers can choose where they live, then why might these knowledge-intensive firms and their workers choose to locate and live in my community?"* The best answers to this polemical question include these phrases: *"enviable quality of life....outstanding public services, especially schools, health care, transportation and airports....enticing career opportunities and good employment mobility....supportive and hospitable environment for entrepreneurs..."*

The firms with the greatest mobility in the future will rate quality—specifically the quality of life in a community—much higher than the cost of location. They will locate where they can attract the best talent. Knowledge workers will locate where they have the greatest career opportunities and superior quality of life.[85] That is exactly what

Carly Fiorina, the President and CEO of Hewlett-Packard Company, said to the nation's governors at the winter 2000 NGA meeting:

> You as Governors are facing the same challenge that we as CEOs are. That is, how to empower your constituents to participate in this new digital economy....A skilled workforce is how you as Governors attract and retain businesses and keep your economies vibrant. And the most skilled workers will drive location decisions and *quality of life is...a key factor for them.* (Emphasis added)[86]

To compete in the 21st century economy, the states and cities must invest strategically to enhance the value of place, which means high quality public services and institutions, mobile and accessible transportation systems, safe and secure communities, and a healthy physical environment. Ross C. DeVol, a researcher at the Milken Institute, who conducted an important study of *America's High-Tech Economy* in 1999, concluded:

> As we enter the age of human capital, where firms merely lease knowledge-assets, firms' location decisions will be increasingly based upon quality-of-life factors that are more important to attracting and retaining this most vital economic asset. In high-tech services, strict business-cost measures will be less important to growing and sustaining technology clusters in metro economies. *Locations that are attractive to knowledge-assets will play a vital role in determining the economic success of regions.* (Emphasis added)[87]

> **Reasons to Enhance the Value of Place**
>
> Regional and national economies are becoming integrated into the global economy. Both international trade and direct foreign investment are growing at a faster rate than world output.
>
> Capital and other factor of production are becoming very mobile. Walter Wriston, former Citibank CEO, has noted, *"Money goes where it is wanted and stays where it is well-treated."*
>
> The digital revolution will enable a growing share of knowledge work to be performed anywhere in the world. Peter Drucker notes, *"Knowledge knows no boundaries."*
>
> The trend of decreasing place-based investments by the federal government will continue to increase the burden on the state and local governments to ensure the economic viability of their communities.

Goal #2: To reengineer state government to become more customer-oriented, market-driven, and dynamic

States have become the "hothouses of experimentation," in the words of Oklahoma Governor Frank Keating. The impressive policy innovation of the state and local governments during the past two decades has been documented by academics,[88] acknowledged by Congress as it devolves more domestic responsibilities to the states, and yet much of the public remains cynical about these governments. Why doesn't the public appreciate how much state and local government operations have improved?

Most citizens have infrequent interactions with government, and frequent contact with firms. Successful firms are constantly innovating and improving; they provide superior services, better quality products, and more consumer choices. Most people are much better off today than they were twenty years ago because science has improved medicine, most products are qualitatively better than they were, and consumer have more choices than they once did.[89] In short, the bar measuring public sector performance has been raised because social expectations are rising. The public expects government to steadily improve its services and operations because it experiences quality improvements daily through the consumption of private-sector's goods and services.

Governors and mayors, in this context, can not be satisfied with the "continuous improvement" of state and city government. If the conventional yardstick for measuring performance in the public sector follows the high marks earned by the most successful firms, then public sector managers must aspire to a much higher quality standard—to "exceed the expectations of the customers." The standard for quality service is now 24–7, not 9 AM to 5 PM Monday through Friday. Pushing these governments to match the quality and performance standards set by leading firms will require the full-time leadership of elected officials and top managers.

The traditional hierarchical organization dominated the 20th century. It was characterized by a single authority at the top; its activities were guided by clear goals and well-defined problems; the role of the manager was to control internal systems; and its management tasks included planning and guiding organizational processes. U.S. manufacturing firms, stunned by rising foreign imports in the 1980s, were among the first to transform how their businesses functioned. They rediscovered *quality*, adopted the mantra of *continuous improvement*, and used *business process reengineering* to recast how work was done. They decentralized operational authority and shifted more responsibilities, including quality management, to their suppliers.

Many of them became *high-performance organizations*, by putting more power in the hands of employees further down the organizational hierarchy, forming teams to organize work, and improving communication throughout the organization. Indeed, one academic study found "average productivity was the highest among firms high in both IT investment and decentralized organization."⁹⁰ Valuable lessons can be learned by public sector managers from the experience of private-sector firms that have used these concepts to transform how work is done.

Despite impressive policy innovation, much of state and local government follows the traditional, hierarchical organizational structure. If telecommunications transcends geography, then information technologies (IT) transform traditional organizational structures. A flood of books written by business consultants offer cutting-edge strategies of how to transform organizations in this digital age. Business executives are learning that the objects of strategy "are held together by a 'glue,' and that glue is essentially information. The glue gets dissolved by new technologies."⁹¹ Put more graphically, John Chambers of Cisco has observed, "There is barely a C.E.O. in the developed world who in the last six months hasn't said to himself, 'Oh, my God! This Internet thing is real. Someone call me an Internet doctor and wire me up.'"⁹²

Transforming How Work is Organized

Some of the most admired companies in businesses far removed from the so-called information industries owe most of their success to their masterful use of information. Toyota built powerful competitive advantages through simultaneous engineering, *kanban*, and quality control—all techniques for processing information. American Airlines used its control of the SABRE reservation system to achieve higher levels of capacity utilization. Wal-Mart exploited its EDI links with suppliers and the logistical technique of cross-docking to achieve dramatic increases in inventory turns. . . . And all the thousands of companies that have embraced Total Quality Management, reengineered their operations, and leveraged their core competencies have chosen to define their managerial goals in terms of flows of information.

Source: Evans & Wurster, *Blown to Bits* (Boston: Harvard Business School Press, 2000), 12.

State and local governments are in the service sector, and they have much to learn about how to organize work from the most innovative firms. Successful firms respond to external threats and robust competition by improving their products, redesigning their operations, and rigorously defining their core competencies. They often seek to form alliances to strengthen their competitive positions, eliminate secondary functions or contract them out to others, and invest in information technologies to transform their organizational structures. Each of these core strategies should be employed by governors and mayors to bring their governments into the digital age.

Redesign State and Local Governments to Exceed the Public's Expectations

The best-selling *Reinventing Government* by Osborne and Gaebler encouraged public sector managers to emphasize consumer service. (Chapter Six was entitled "Customer-Driven Government: Meeting the Needs of the Customer, Not the Bureaucracy.")[93] This is an important mission that bears continued emphasis. Borrowing from private-sector lessons, a business consultant might offer three general principles to create a customer-oriented emphasis throughout state and local government:

- Understand the process used to do daily tasks;
- Invest in new communications technologies to improve operations and services; and
- Change the organizational culture to make the provision of quality services to the public the top priority.

The first step is often underappreciated. Change agents sometimes leap into new technology without fully understanding the current processes of work in state government. This leap leads to "paving the cow path" according to Hammer and Champy, experts in reengineering the business process.[94] From their perspective, making incremental improvements falls far short of success. Indeed, Jerry Mechling, a Kennedy School professor at Harvard University, provides this explanation for focusing on the radical redesign of work in the public sector:

> Reengineering is radical change. It is the fundamental redesign of work processes, often enabled by the aggressive use of information technologies, and intended to bring about rapid improvement. It rarely happens. These days all sorts of projects are called "reengineering." Most aren't. True reengineering means:

Fundamental change.
Rapid progress toward radical goals.
Selective use of appropriate information technology.[95]

State Government as a Legacy System

IT people struggle with a terrible headache called "legacy systems": enormous information architectures, with layer upon layer of improvements, extensions, and investments, that turn out to be massively inferior to a simple, clean, new box. Beyond a certain point, the problems of updating and maintaining compatibility become so severe that it makes sense to junk the entire system and start from scratch. Business systems are *human* software: they follow exactly the same logic. There are legacy organizations, legacy mindsets, legacy competencies. And beyond a certain point it is necessary to junk *them* and start again.

Source: Evans and Wurster, *Blown to Bits: How the New Economics of Information Transforms Strategies* (Boston: Harvard Business School Press, 2000), 227.

The governors and mayors must be leaders in these three activities—to improve the process of how government does its business to exceed the public's expectations; to implement new technologies to improve its operations and services; and, especially, to lead the required changes in organizational culture to put customer service as the first priority of state government.

State and local governments committed to serving its citizens as valued customers will design a host of communications systems to ensure that every interaction "exceeds the expectations of the consumer." In practical terms, this means that automated telephone answering systems will be scrapped in favor of courteous, well-informed operators who can direct most inquires to the appropriate agency or desk. Another example of treating the citizen as valued customer would be to design the state's web page to provide easy access to the information most frequently sought. Public sector organizations in the 21st century will need multiple service delivery systems: both "high tech and high touch," to borrow John Naisbitt's phrase.

The first wave of web sites produced by state governments provided scant information of most value, except to foreign visitors planning their visit to the states. The social learning curve has advanced rapidly with this technology. States and cities can now borrow generously from private sector innovations in designing web pages to answer the most frequently asked questions about their governments, their regulations on business and the environment, their laws, and their most popular services.[96]

Use IT to Transform How the Business of Government is Performed

Governor Jim Geringer of Wyoming, a former engineer, observed, "We once thought of computers as a way of automating operations, but today information technologies can transform how we deliver services in the future." State and local governments, as laboratories of democracy, have been the leaders in innovating with some technologies such as distance learning, information kiosks, electronic commerce, geographic information systems (GIS), electronic bracelets to monitor parolees, intelligent transportation systems (ITS) that improve highway and transit operations, electronic tolls to reduce traffic congestion, and a host of others.

Washington state is generally acknowledged to be the leading state government in converting labor-intensive operations into electronic systems. Virtually every state can boast about its innovative achievements: Oregon was the first to use electronic communication to present bids and solicit vendors for state contracts; Info/Texas provided a statewide network of information kiosks that provide basic information, in English and Spanish, about state services and employment opportunities; Utah enacted the first digital signature law; Arizona and Massachusetts enable electronic renewal of driver's licenses; the Oklahoma Tax Commission launched the nation's first online electronic filing program; North Carolina and Vermont require teachers and high school graduates to prove IT competency; Virginia's Commission for Information Technology developed several innovative policies (including a way to grapple with the problem of unsolicited commercial e-mail, called spam); and a growing number of states are beginning to issue other permits and licenses electronically.[97]

A Digital States survey conducted by The Center for Digital Government and the Progress and Freedom Foundation concluded that "Georgia, Alaska, Washington, Kansas and Wisconsin make all necessary license and permit forms available online."[98] These are notable successes, but this glass is not even close to being half full. Technology represents approximately ten percent of the average state budget. Half of the states do not have a designated Chief Information Officer reporting directly to the governor. In most of those states, IT budgets are allocated to each agency, which have independent IT directors and data centers. Former state CIOs lament about "working with divided authority and locking horns with independent agency heads."[99]

What might 21ˢᵗ Century Digital Government Look Like?

A couple expecting twins and planning to renovate their home will use their television to submit and receive all the necessary plans and permits electronically via e-mail and the Internet. There will be no need to take time off from work or to devote precious Saturday mornings or family evenings to visit their town hall, planning board, building inspector, or zoning commission.

An enterprising young man who wants to open a lakeside restaurant catering to boaters will use his home PC to apply for all the business permits he needs in one sitting through one World Wide Web site—despite the fact that his business is of concern to the state and local health departments, Federal and state tax agencies, the state environmental protection commission, the labor department, and local zoning and economic development officials.

A government disaster response coordinator will use wireless communications, multimedia analytical tools, and dynamic and static geographic data from Federal, state, local, and private sources to direct a massive recovery effort following a devastating ice storm. These integrated and constantly updated information sources will help restore bridges, roads, power grids, telecommunications services, water supplies, health care facilities, homes, farms, schools, and businesses.

Source: Sharon S. Dawes et al, *Some Assembly Required: Building a Digital Government for the 21ˢᵗ Century*, Center for Technology in Government, SUNY at Albany, NY, March 1999.

This lack of coordination in IT investment and planning is a searing indictment of "business as usual" in state governments. To be charitable, it suggests that some governors, state legislators, and top managers just "do not get it." They do not appreciate the tremendous potential of information technologies to transform how work can be done, resulting in superior services, greater efficiencies, and more productivity.

The public sector lags far behind leading corporations in exploiting the Internet and implementing digital technologies to transform how the public's work is performed. There are important reasons for this lag. First, the competitive pressure on firms to innovate is extreme. Second, all bureaucracies resist change. Third, most public sector organizations cling to the hierarchical organizational structure, have annual budget cycles for spending authorizations, and are led by senior managers socialized to minimize risk. This organizational culture does not encourage experimentation or nurture innovation. (For a path out of this dysfunctional maze, see "Reforming State Procurement to Buy the Best Information Technology Solution," (available at <www.nga.org/pubs/issuebriefs/1999/sum990809itprocurement.asp>).

Fourth, the private sector is rapidly bidding away scarce talent from state and local governments. The scarcity of qualified technology workers and the growing demand for them has created a serious problem in the public sector. An estimated twenty percent of the computer and telecommunications jobs in California state government are unfilled. The proximity of the state capitol to Silicon Valley—the greatest concentration of technology talent in the world—does not alleviate this problem, but heightens the irony. "Californians can't yet use the World Wide Web to renew their vehicle registration. Nor can they buy a fishing license online. They can't even check a central Web site where the state's computer jobs are posted because such a site doesn't exist." One state official laments, "We are running the danger of converting the state into a giant Dilbert cartoon."[100]

Many in state government are frustrated by the inability to move current operations and public services rapidly into the digital age. North Carolina Lt. Governor Dennis Wicker said, "What has emerged from public surveys was a demand for a Web site which was user-friendly, simple and easy to use. Citizens want to use credit and debit cards to do business with the state, and they want an electronic shop front oriented to them, as users, not to the state's organizational structure." NC Secretary of State Elaine Marshall echoed this sentiment:

> People want ease of access in government. They are not interested in which agency handles which service. Citizens are frustrated by the internal silo effect. In addition, they

want all factual information available online, but do not want government to lose the human touch.

Many government services are already available online, but more are on the way. Our customers can use information made available on the Internet 24 hours a day, seven days a week, 365 days a year. We cannot continue to tell people their government only works 8 to 5, five days a week. We must provide them with some other options for service.[101]

Promoting Digital Government

Think customer, not government agency. Digital government is all about being customer-focused. Too often, public agencies organize services and programs according to a political or bureaucratic logic. In contrast, the Internet enables the seamless integration of government services organized around what citizens need.

Focus on digital transactions between citizens and government. Net-enabled government services should be a key driver in government reengineering efforts.

Pass savings on to citizens by offering rebates or discounts for interacting with government electronically. Digital government can generate significant savings for government, and in order to encourage citizens to use these low-cost systems, government should pass some of the savings back to them.

Invest money now to save money tomorrow. Elected officials and agency heads often view spending on digital government as simply one more item competing with others for limited funds. In fact, because they cut costs, expenditures on digital government usually pay for themselves in relatively short periods of time.

Source: Atkinson et al, *The State New Economic Index*, Progressive Policy Institute, July 1999, 29.

The public sector is constrained by inflexible pay schedules and fossilized hiring rules. If state governments were to borrow from the play book of successful firms, they would not hesitate to negotiate with private vendors to build and manage the advanced information technology systems required to bring operations and services into the digital age. As innovative firms demonstrate, the fastest way to create a new system is to find a qualified vendor to built it. That is how DeKalb County in Georgia entered the digital future and created its version of e-government. The Commissioners wanted to put the county government online—and enable the 554,000 residents to use the Internet to pay property taxes, register automobiles, and transact business with the county government. The county did not try to build the infrastructure or design the applications. Instead, it selected a private vendor to build the system. The public gets information for free, and it gets e-government. The vendor gets a transaction fee on bill paying transactions. Elizabeth Wasserman, writing in *The Industry Standard*, summarizes this approach: "Governments that want to go online without hitting up taxpayers are working with firms that exchange Web work for transaction fees."[102] The National Information Consortium, Ezgov.com, and e-gov.com are few vendors entering this market to assist public sector agencies move into electronic government quickly.

Organizations or Markets?

Governors, county executives, and mayors need to ask which are the best tools to use to provide public services and perform the business of government. Both traditional hierarchical organizations and markets have admirable virtues and serious limitations. Evans and Wurster, business consultants, draw this sharp distinction:

> Hierarchies encourage *collaboration*: people within an organization are able to work together without having to negotiate responsibilities and rewards in great detail beforehand, because it is their common employer who bears the risk....Hierarchies are amenable to leadership and to strategy. Markets, in general, are not...They evolve more like biological systems...They follow their noses: each evolutionary step that proves a success encourages the next.[103]

No clear decision rule has emerged yet in either the public or private sectors. The toughest decisions in both spheres involve the crucial tradeoff between retaining daily control of operations by directing managing organizations or outsourcing activities that the market can provide more cost-effectively than the organization can produce internally. As discussed above, this tension reflects the insights of Ronald Coase, who first asked why production is usually organized within the firm. Business theory is now focused on these "make versus buy" decisions. Organizational leaders "decide which aspects of their operations they handle internally (incurring coordination costs) and which they decide to buy (incurring transaction costs)."[104]

This underlying theory of transaction costs provides some guidance as public sector managers search for more effective means to conduct the public's business. History buffs will recall that FDR wanted to create the Tennessee Valley Authority, in part, to serve as a public benchmark against which to evaluate the performance of the dominant investor-owned utilities that dominated electric generation in the 1930s. Seven decades later, that history has been turned upside down: state and local governments are increasingly choosing to privatize operations and services that had been provided almost exclusively by public agencies. Part of this experimentation reflects a desire to obtain private sector benchmarks against which to evaluate public sector performance.

Privatization, as defined by John Donahue, a professor at the Kennedy School of Government at Harvard University, is "the practice of delegating public duties to *private* organization." Donahue makes three significant observations: 1. The term is not new; it was first used by Peter Drucker in 1968; 2. "Large fractions of federal, state, and local budgets have always gone to purchase goods and services from outside governments;" and 3. Controversy on this approach accelerated during the 1980s when ideological conservatives linked privatization with their desire to reduce the scope and size of government. Donahue proposes two sober tests to guide this important decision about public or private:

> The first dimension concerns *financing*: Should we pay for some good or service individually, out of our own resources, or should we pay for it collectively with funds raised through one form or another of taxation? The second dimension concerns *performance*: Should the good be produced or the service delivered by a governmental organization or by a nongovernmental organization?[105]

The Privatization Controversy

Proponents of privatization believe private enterprise can deliver the same services government provides for less money, with higher quality of service and increased flexibility. Opponents of privatization believe that such efforts undermine the quality of services, destroy public employee unions, invite corruption, and weaken government control of services key to the public interest. The privatization debate reflects basic questions about the general philosophy and role of government. Are there certain needs, such as public safety or the dispensation of justice, that should be met only by government? Can government be "run more like a business," and if so, how? Should government subject itself to competition in providing services?

Source: *An Action Agenda to Redesign State Government*, National Governors' Association, 1993, xii.

Michigan Governor John Engler directed his top managers to employ a similar process for evaluating how state government should be managed and which functions could be eliminated, reduced, or contracted to private firms. The process was called PERM, representing these policy options: privatize, eliminate, retain (in its current form), and modify.[106] Several states, including Massachusetts, borrowed this construct from Michigan during the mid-1990s to guide their efforts to evaluate various activities. Following Michigan's example, they used this paradigm as the context for the giving a close scrutiny to their state government operations, especially traditional activities that had seldom been questioned.

Contemporary efforts to privatize public functions and services yield an observation about process and a related philosophical concern. Steve Goldsmith was an acknowledged leader in using privatization during his years as Mayor of Indianapolis. Some of the lessons from his experience merit careful consideration:

> 1. *Let public employees bid against private firms for public contracts.* In the first four years, the city held 64 public-private competitions (valued at more than $500 million) and the public workers won 16 bids and split another 13 bids with private contractors. In their eagerness to win these bids, the workers convinced top managers to reform organizational rules and eliminate middle managers, both of which improved their efficiency. This story demonstrates that "good people are trapped in bad systems," as the advocates of reinventing government often contend.
>
> 2. *Maintain the credibility of the competitive bidding process.* David Osborne and Peter Plastrik suggest establishing "control over the bidding process to a neutral, nonpolitical party—for example, a civil servant auditor or purchasing chief. You should not let the government organization performing the services control the bidding process."[107]
>
> 3. *Establish performance measures to enrich the managers' knowledge about the tasks to be bid competitively.* Goldsmith has spoken openly about the need to analyze the hard costs of certain functions prior to the competitive

bidding process. "How can managers seek competitive bids from private contractors to fill street pot holes without first knowing what it actually costs?" asks Goldsmith.

Performance measures should be established on every function and activity of state government, regardless of where and how it may be performed. Harry Hatry of the Urban Institute defines performance measures as *"measurement on a regular basis of the results (outcomes) and efficiency of services or programs."*[108] These measures serve as important benchmarks—an essential tool used by leading firms to monitor performance against their competitors and the best in the world. Benchmarking in the public sector provides important information about which functions or activities should be retained inside state government and which ones outsourced. It is also essential for monitoring the performance of firms doing work under contract for the public sector. Privatization does not diminish government's responsibility to monitor and supervise contracted work. Performance-based accountability must accompany privatization.

> **Measuring Inputs and Outcomes**
>
> "When you can measure what you are speaking about, and express it in numbers, you know something about it; but when you cannot measure it, when you cannot express it in numbers, your knowledge is of a meager and unsatisfactory kind."— Lord Kelvin

Privatization is not a panacea for reforming the public sector. (Indeed, Frank O'Brannon beat Goldsmith in the 1996 Indiana gubernatorial race.) When done in a deliberate fashion, it has proven to be an effective means of obtaining goods and services for the public. Combined with performance measures and a neutral bidding process, it can produce tangible public savings and stimulate the transformation of public sector organizations.

Using Competition and Community to Provide Public Services

Traditionally, policy debates have been defined by budget decisions about resource allocation. How much, for example, does the public sector invest in traditional institutions committed to serving the public? Future policy debates should not be limited to "how much to spend?" but on *how to spend these public dollars to achieve the best results.*

John E. Brandl, a 12-year veteran of the Minnesota legislature, has written a thoughtful critique of how most policy discussions are focused on inputs, rather than results. He comments, "If more dollars are appropriated to education (or welfare or highways or whatever), corresponding and appropriate outcomes will occur more frequently. That theory lies behind politicians' pledges of more funds to this or that project as a sign of determination to generate better results." Brandl proposes two constructs as the basis for redesigning policy approaches and delivery systems:

> Harnessing self-interest through competition—choice, and...encouraging affiliations that inspire altruistic behavior—community. Successful production of services depends on one or both....Competition and community do not substitute for government. They are the instruments through which government facilitates the working out of public purposes by a free people.[109]

"Pay as you throw" fees for household garbage collection might seem like a trivial example of using markets instead of command-and-control environmental policies—it is not. In 1991, the Seattle City Council initiated charges based on how much waste was left for municipal workers to collect. Within eight years, more than four thousand cities have adopted "pay as you throw" charges. Virginia Postrel, a writer who advocates dynamist policies, explains:

Instead of a flat fee regardless of how much they throw out, which tends to encourage more garbage, residents pay a per-bag charge that captures the real disposal costs. Pay-as-you-throw cuts garbage generation by 10 percent or more. But unlike recycling mandates or materials bans, it does not tell people what choices they must make.[110]

Markets, if structured carefully, can provide choice in the distribution of public benefits (via housing vouchers), provide goods and services to the public sector (as with privatization), and achieve important social objectives (e.g., market-based incentives for environmental protection). The use of markets is a powerful tool for the public sector. Consider these possibilities: "Pay as you throw" fees for household garbage collection, congestion pricing of rush hour traffic instead of HOV lanes, the "buy and preserve" option that allows developers to get building permits after ensuring that neighboring wetlands and habitats for endangered species were protected, and variations of the air emissions trading scheme as a substitute for the traditional permitting process of the traditional command and control regime.

The next wave of policy innovation will draw upon these approaches. Together, they could shift state and local governments away from being the primary provider/ producer/builder/manager for every kind of public services. The artful use of markets to distribute public goods, achieve social outcomes, and produce services to meet the changing needs of the public requires skilled managers to negotiate, bargain and monitor performance. The skills required have less in common with those perfected by most production managers, and are much more like being the conductor of an orchestra. "Steering rather than rowing" was the memorable phrase by Osborne and Gaebler in their best-selling *Reinventing Government*.[111]

Public-Private Partnerships

America is a mobile society. Just sixty percent of the population currently lives in the state in which they were born. In a fluid society, fewer people today are as committed to their physical community as they once were. Furthermore, the federal government has been shifting its investment strategy toward domestic programs that serve people (regardless of where they live) and less and less in place-based economic development. Federal grants-in-aid to state and local governments averaged 21.5 percent of their total spending over the 1990–1995 period. This is well below the 26.5 percent peak that occurred in 1978.[112]

The state and local governments will have to do more with their own resources. Who cares as much as elected state officials about maintaining the economic viability of their communities and their state? Who else remains linked, as governments are, to geography? The private sector, especially the small business community, has invested in communities, earns their living from them, and has often demonstrated leadership in addressing important social problems. These governments should form partnerships with business associations to guide future job training initiatives and to build upon their collective economic strengths.

Network Governance

The last strategy borrowed from the business world that can be used to transform how state and local governments function is called network governance. The premise is that government is just one actor in our pluralistic society, yet the most pressing problems confronting society require a collaborative response. Reducing teenage pregnancy, increasing adult literacy, promoting life-long learning, expanding economic opportunities to disadvantaged populations, reducing substance abuse by youth and adults—these are social problems beyond the capacity of state and local governments to adequately solve by themselves. Programs financed through the public sector often achieve modest success on their own, given the magnitude and complexity of these challenges. Complex social problems require comprehensive responses by other key social institutions and their leaders. Building an effective collaboration is the first step. Building a process for governance decision-making is next. Third is designing a structure to guide collaborative action to address mutually defined problems.

Organizational Models for the 21st Century

	Rational Organization	*Network Governance*
Actors	Organization as coherent units with clear purposes	Organizations as part of a network of organizations
Processes	Rational, structured from top, directed towards goals and highest highest possible output; Planning, organizing and controlling	Frequent interactions and resource exchanges; Guided by links between organizations
Decisions	Result of strategic actions of central authority Aimed at reaching goals	Result of negotiations between organizations; Aimed at sustaining resources
Power	Clear, centralized authority structure (Top of organization)	No central authority structure Power depends on resources
Information/ Values	Scientific way of gathering information Clear goals and values	Information possessed by different actors Values are conflicting

Source: Adapted from E. H. Klign, "Policy networks: An Overview," *Managing Complex Networks: Strategies for the Public Sector*, edited by Walter J.M. Kickert, Erik-Hans Klijn and Joop F. M. Koppenjan (London: Sage Publications, 1997), Table 2-2, 20.

Individual firms form business alliances to develop new products, capture market share, and create competitive advantages. State and local governments have always worked closely with other social institutions. Network governance is distinguished from traditional collaborative efforts by shared decision making, decentralized power, dispersed information, and multiple actors working on mutually defined problems. It requires, like all collaborative efforts, trust among the participants and clear mutual objectives. If it can be sustained, network governance has the potential to make substantial social change—far beyond the power of any independent actor acting alone. The Internet evolved rapidly into a worldwide communications medium, in part, because the early pioneers developed a common protocol. No single organization—not AT&T, not the federal government—could have designed, constructed, and build what has become the Internet. Its astounding success illustrates the untouchable potential of network governance.[113]

Leadership is Hard Work

Mark Twain once wrote that if all you have is a hammer, then everything looks like nails. Top managers in state and local governments often see their agency as the hammer, and their mission as nailing everything in sight. Managers of hierarchical organizations like to retain control of their operations; they have been socialized to do this throughout their long and productive careers in public service. Requiring them to attend a management seminar on the virtues of delegating authority to others or learning about how to share power with colleagues is not going to change the organization culture of a public agency. TQM was a benign fad while it lasted.

These strategies to improve how public organizations function represent hard work. The strategies of putting the customer first, implementing IT to transform how the public's work is performed, using privatization to obtain goods and services, and experimenting with new approaches to use the community and develop market-based instruments to achieve social outcomes are challenging endeavors. Forming effective partnerships and collaborations with other social institutions take time and sustained effort to produce significant results. The common thread among these approaches is the search to improve the core competencies of state and local government to respond to changing social needs and enhance the economic vitality of our communities.

If the greatest insight of the conservative critics of government is that pouring more tax dollars into dysfunctional bureaucracies and poorly designed programs does not always significantly improve social outcomes, then the greatest insight of the liberals is that government can be used responsibly to expand educational and economic opportunities to those left behind. And moderates of both political philosophies understand that the process of how we govern ourselves in a democracy has social value, affecting the level of citizenship, civility, civil engagement, and social trust. Robert Putnam, a professor at Harvard University, describes *social capital* as "connections among individuals—social networks and the norms of reciprocity and trustworthiness that arise from them." Indeed, proponents of this concept suggest that "Communities and regions rich in social capital suffer less crime, educate their children better, and have more smoothly functioning economies—or so the theory goes."[114]

Government has core competencies. They are articulated in the U.S. Constitution—"establish Justice, insure domestic Tranquility, provide for the common defense, promote the general Welfare, and secure the Blessing of Liberty to ourselves and our Posterity," and so on. Which strategies will prove most effective in enhancing the core competencies of your state and local governments?

The threshold test of any innovative strategy is its ability to preserve the integrity of government, and improving its credibility with the general public. In a democratic society, governments and the people are sovereign. They each have rights and responsibilities—both independent of each other and to each other. The public is more than an undifferentiated mass of customers served by public sector organizations; they are citizens to whom government must be held responsible and accountable. Citizens in a democracy must have opportunities to express their views about the public's business. Government must have an open process for engaging the public to debate social priorities and the best means to achieve meaningful results.

Governors and mayors can liberally borrow from private sector experiments in transforming how work can be performed, but the business of government—the public's business—must always be done in an open process. This process distinction makes the public sector unique from the private realm. The loudest voices for "making government run like a business" seldom appreciate this fundamental difference. Public policies are debated openly in state legislatures and city councils; business decisions can be made in corporate boardrooms behind closed doors. Professor Sayre made this point some years ago, when he quipped, "There are many, many similarities between public administration and business management, and all of them are trivial."[115]

The Art of Public Management

Proposition One: "There are many, many similarities between public administration and business management, and all of them are trivial," says Professor Wally Sayre.

Proposition Two: Leaders in public sector organizations can learn from the most innovative firms about using IT to improve services and operations, achieving greater efficiency and effectiveness.

Proposition Three: The creative tension, the apparent paradox, between the first two statements defines the "art" of public sector management at the cusp of the 21st century.

Every elected official respects the public and value its voice in democratic decision making. They should articulate a vision for transforming how the public's business can be performed better, quickly, faster. Fundamental changes in public sector organizations are required. Governors and mayors must lead. The public must be engaged in this process of experimenting with new approaches to respond to social problems and improving social outcomes.

> **Strategies to transform the work of state and local government:**
>
> *Change the organizational culture to put customer service first. Citizens may require multiple delivery systems: both "high tech and high touch."*
>
> *Implement information technologies to transform core functions of government and improve public services.*
>
> *Develop performance measures for every government activity and function.*
>
> *Establish benchmarks to compare the public sector performance against neighboring state governments.*
>
> *Use both measures to determine which functions should be retained within state government and which should be outsourced via a competitive bidding process.*
>
> *Contract with private vendors to build digital age systems (e-government) if it proves difficult to develop them internally.*
>
> *Develop market policy instruments to achieve social outcomes to replace heavy-handed command and control regulation. And,*
>
> *Build private-public partnerships and other collaborative efforts to achieve meaningful results on intractable social problems.*

Goal #3: To make strategic investments to build the intellectual and physical infrastructure needed in the New Economy

The term "human capital" was coined by Nobel Laureate economist Theodore Schultz in his 1961 book, *Investing in Ourselves*, in which he "argued that investments in education and skills were as important, if not more important than investments in physical capital for less-developed countries."[116] Management expert Peter Drucker made the same assessment:

> A little reflection will show that the rate of capital formation to which economists give so much attention is a secondary factor....The basic factor in an economy's development must

be the rate at which a country produces people with imagination and vision, education, theoretical and analytical skills.[117]

In 1990 the National Center on Education and the Economy published a report with an ominous title: *America's Choice: high skills or low wages!* This report argued that the numerous deficiencies in the nation's education and training systems, especially compared with those of our strongest economic competitors, were undermining our prospects for future prosperity. The report recommended establishing new educational performance standards for all students, developing a system of technical and professional training opportunities for non-college-bound youth; and encouraging employers to invest in additional training programs for their workers. A similar analysis was offered by the *Wall Street Journal*:

> Jobs are becoming more demanding, more complex. But our schools don't seem up to the task. They are producing students who lack the skills that business so desperately needs to compete in today's global economy. And in doing so, they are condemning students to a life devoid of meaningful employment.[118]

In *America and the New Economy*, Anthony Carnevale observed:

> Despite flat overall wage growth, there have been dramatic shifts in earnings among different groups of Americans. Wage increases in the new economy are rationed with an increasingly uneven hand, resulting in a growing maldistribution of income in the United States. More now than ever, *learning is the rationing hand that distributes earnings in the American economy. People with the most education and access to learning on the job are doing best; those with the least education and least access to learning on the job are doing worst.* (Emphasis added.)[119]

The states have been active on many fronts in the decade since these ominous "calls to action" were issued. But the glass remains half empty. If much of our success as a society can be attributed to the expansive opportunities provided to the many throughout our national history, then the strategy for future social progress lies in expanding opportunity further—to those who have been left behind, or need a helping hand. Consider the issue of how society rations its investment in young people. Government spends a tremendous sum in assisting higher education, which benefits society and those fortunate to attend these schools. In 1994, an estimated 36.5 percent of young adults from low-income families had not enrolled in postsecondary education, compared to 20.7 percent of middle-income students, and just 6.9 percent of students from high-income families.[120] The public sector can and should do a better job of expanding educational and economic opportunity.

Elected officials must continue their efforts to improve public institutions and enable them to adapt to changing social needs. They must also explore alternative arrangements to promote life-long learning. Now that knowledge has become a prominent factor of production in the new economy, governments must become flexible and creative about nurturing social investments in human capital in innovative ways.

Under the umbrella of promoting life-long learning, the best public sector investment is in babies, infants, and young children (up to age 3) who have tremendous learning abilities if they are well-fed, stimulated, and loved. The scientific research on infant brain development (up to age 2) is compelling. Some states have begun new programs to provide early childhood interventions, especially in disadvantaged households, to ensure that young children receive the enriched support that will enhance their ability to learn, thrive and prosper throughout their lives.[121] There are moral and economic reasons for states to make these investments in early childhood interventions. Children raised in disadvantaged families often become troubled teenagers and adults, imposing social costs and personal hardships on their families.

Improve Educational Institutions (K-18)

Since the mid-1970s when the courts began to rule on school equalization cases, the states have steadily increased their share of the cost of public education. This has been good policy and good politics. In the last decade, a process for establishing standards for public schools has received substantial attention, which most Governors have supported. Reducing class size is another experiment that may improve educational achievement, especially in the early grades. Many states—Texas, Michigan, Florida, and California—have sought to deregulate state educational policy, shedding laws and regulations that had the effect of micro-managing the classrooms. State deregulation of educational policy might provide more autonomy to the average teacher if superintendents and principals also accept the logic of decentralizing operational and instructional decisions.

Each of these policy approaches has merit. More state funding to equalize educational opportunity is a good strategy, although state policy makers are just as susceptible to educational fads as are teachers and local school boards. (How was Outcome Based Education different from the preceding philosophy?) Establishing standards for public schools is an equally fine strategy—every public service should have performance standards so the providers can benchmark their activities for comparison with other providers. But if teachers are encouraged to teach to the standardized test, then performance soars—until the test is changed. And, what happens if a school does not measure up to the rising norm: does it get more resources to enrich its educational program? Failure in the public sector must some consequence.

The charter school movement shows some promise for improving educational outcomes. Following the lead of Minnesota in

1991, 32 states have enacted charter legislation which enables public funding to be given to schools managed by someone other the local school board. A few Governors have boldly explored educational voucher systems, believing that introducing parental choice may be an another way of strengthening education and making the public school bureaucracy more responsive. Governor Jeb Bush in Florida signed a limited voucher plan in the summer of 1999. The voucher idea represents even greater potential for creating sweeping organizational changes that may be necessary for substantial gains in educational achievement. Most important, though, it would enable educators to create schools on a human scale, which foster a sense of community and facilitate learning.

> ### The Changing Needs of Children and Society
>
> For the first time in a century, reformers are beginning to think "outside the box" of the industrial-era factory model of schooling. There is a growing recognition that one-size-fits-all education does not fit everyone, and that schooling must be adaptive to the changing needs of children and society....That hierarchical system served the nation well for many years, but over time it became more rigid, more inefficient, and less able to provide equal educational opportunity. It is not up to the challenges of the new century, nor is it capable of achieving the high standard of universal literacy that a modern economy and advanced society demand.
>
> **Source:** Diane Ravitch and Joseph P. Viteritti, "Introduction," *New Schools for a New Century* (New Haven, CT: Yale University Press, 1997), 1.

The harshest critique of the *American High School Today* must begin with James Conant's book (of that title) published in 1959. His book was earnest, thoughtful, constructive, and wise. Conant, a former president of Harvard University, proposed creating a system of comprehensive high schools. The issue is not the merits of his book or recommendations, but its power as the guiding light for educators. It was revered. For the next five decades, educators used Conant's book as the blueprint—the *one, best way to build high schools across America*. Educators are excellent advocates for what they think is best for their students (even when it happens to benefits themselves). "If we had just one high school in the county, we could teach Sanscrit!" gushed a Vermont educator in the 1960s. Policy makers deferred to the professionals; the educators won. It was the best of intentions. They got most of what they wanted: physical plants so large, so impersonal that they resemble the Toyota factory in Lexington, KY that produces the best-selling Camry.

Learning is a human activity. Most learn through instruction; many learn by doing or by example. Some, if sufficiently motivated, can learn by themselves. Most benefit by learning in a community of peers. Some can learn in a factory setting. Others can not. The best educators do their best in this impersonal setting; others do not. This is the critique of Diane Ravitch, a educational historian:

> The "shopping mall high school"...offers something for everyone, cafeteria-style, but it cannot provide the individual support and nurturance that most of these young people need. The typical comprehensive high school is large and impersonal, with a studied air of neutrality toward all students. But that is exactly what these children do not need. They need schools that work closely with each student and his or her family; they need schools that are designed to be intensely engaged with each child as a unique person. *Children need schools where they are many adults who know their names and care about them, know when they are absent, know when they have a problem, think about their futures, and expect to talk frequently to their parents or guardians.*[122] (Emphasis added)

How do we create a system of schools that is dynamic, diverse, performance-based, and accountable—one that is supportive of professionals, responsive to the community, engaging to parents, stimulating to students, intolerant of failure and intolerance, and committed to excellence? To transpose a John Dewey quote, "The community should want for all of its children what the wisest and most loving parents want for their children." Which of these reforms—more state funding, standards for educational outcomes, smaller class size, state deregulation—would move us closest to these aspirations?

High school, during the industrial era, was the endpoint of formal education for most workers. Today, in the New Economy, high school is simply the foundation for future learning. It is not an endpoint at all, it is still at the beginning of one's lifetime of learning. The goal of public education was once to prepare youth to become productive citizens and assume adult responsibilities. *In a knowledge-based economy, the only thing any high school student needs to learn is how to learn.* In the New Economy, skill sets erode overnight as new technology emerges, jobs churn quickly and without warning, and new responsibilities will require constant learning.

Making better use of educational institutions to help adults learn is only one strategy to assist lifelong learning, which will grow in importance as the pace of change accelerates in this New Economy. Here is an important historical perspective:

> Learning in agricultural economies is often church led, focuses on children between 7 and 14 years of age, and is sufficient to last all the years of a working life. In industrial economies, learning has been government led, and the age range of students is between 5 and 22. *In knowledge economies, the rapid pace of technological change means that learning must be constant and that education must be updated throughout one's working life. People have to increase their learning power to sustain their earning power.*

Knowledge is doubling every seven years, and in technical fields in particular, half of what students learn in their first year of college is obsolete by the time they graduate. In the labor force, the need to keep pace with technological change is felt even more acutely. For companies to remain competitive, and for workers to stay employable, they must continue to learn.[123] (Emphasis added)

Expanding job training opportunities to the broader population

Lifetime employment at one firm is a relic of the past—a characteristic of the old economy. The *Wall Street Journal* reports that job churning—the combination of new job creation from startups and job destruction from business failure—is accelerating.[124] The Progressive Policy Institute includes job churning as an indicator of the economic dynamism of a state's economy.[125]

States and cities need to redesign social institutions to provide opportunities for everyone for life-long learning. For two decades, much of the public investment in job training has been targeted to the most disadvantaged workers, which has been both hard to do well and difficult to defend to a skeptical public. This remains an important challenge, but the public sector must expand far beyond that limited objective. The competitive pressure of the global economy and the premium attached to computing and analytical skills should encourage policy makers to redesign training programs for youth and adults in a variety of institutional settings, including the public schools.

Some of the strongest advocates for new initiatives to promote life-long learning in our society present solutions that do not match the social challenge. They call for bold new apprenticeship programs in the high schools, new workforce training programs for displaced workers, and new educational entitlements for adults. Each approach has merit, yet none is the panacea. Indeed, this policy challenge should elicit creative approaches and experimentation.

Policy makers should be guided by three common sense principles:

1. New workforce training programs should incorporate performance measures. The Employment Training Panel in California may be among the most productive and effective state training programs in the country for two reasons: its training programs are designed for experienced workers and it uses tough performance standards. According to one evaluation, the panel "requires that each trainee land a job using his [her] new skills and hold that job at least 90 days. If not, the state takes back all the money it paid to train him [her]— even if the trainee dies...70 percent of the participants fulfill the state's requirements."[126]

2. Work experience in the private sector provides valuable skills. With this salient example, a sociologist takes issue with the view that society only benefits from activities supported by governments:

> More than 20,000,000 members of the current American labor force have worked at one of McDonald's 8,000 restaurants, mostly at slightly better than minimum-wage entry-level jobs. McDonald's does not think of itself as a training ground where egocentric teenagers, including dropouts, can learn the sorts of skills and values that will enable them to move on to better jobs; but its more successful at doing so than most governmentally sponsored training programs. Unfortunately, Americans wax nostalgic over disappearing work experiences for children—e.g., paper routes and family farms—while they ignore the large fast-food chains that provide training in crucial work skills, like getting to work on time, being well groomed, working hard and fast.[127]

3. *The public sector objective should be to expand learning opportunities for all citizens. Individuals will always retain personal responsibilities to invest in themselves by obtaining more education and pursuing new learning opportunities.* This important distinction suggests that Individual Development Accounts, patterned after IRAs, might be the most promising path to expand learning opportunities. Government can match personal contributions for low-income adults to their IDAs; any individual could later use those savings as a voucher to obtain more education or more skills training as he or she chooses. An IDA program, partially subsidized by government for the poor, is empowering. It would expand educational and economic opportunities to many who have been left behind.[128]

Strategies to promote life-long learning:

Investing in early childhood programs because brain development research indicates that enriched learning at the beginning of life is extremely important.

Continuing to improve educational outcomes in the public school system by using a variety of levers—establishing standards, deregulating state regulations, reducing class size in the lower grades—and promoting alternative approaches such as charter schools.

Forming public-private partnerships with industry associations to administer skill-based training programs.

Redesigning job training programs to achieve better results and more accountability—by providing vouchers to individuals and paying providers based on their success in placing (and retaining) workers in jobs for which they are qualified. And,

Providing public grants to match personal savings by low-income workers in Individual Development Accounts.

Strategic Public Infrastructure Investment

Throughout our nation's history, public leaders expressed their unbounded confidence in the future by investing in public infrastructure. We enjoy the legacy of their foresight. The authors of the U.S. Constitution understood the value of transportation and communications networks to weave the states together as a nation—Section 8, defining Congressional powers, includes "To establish Post Offices and post Roads." As an agrarian nation, the states built roads and canals and encouraged the development of railroads to facilitate the movement of goods to markets. Following this leadership, the federal government supported the development of Samuel Morse's telegraph experiment, and joined the states in promoting the development of a national railroad system. These communications and transportation networks fostered the development of national markets for the goods produced in the industrial era. National advertising followed the diffusion of radio as popular entertainment in the 1920s, another major step toward creating national markets.

Prudent infrastructure investment is essential for economic growth, but indiscriminate public investment sometimes causes unintended consequences. The Interstate Highway Defense Act, adopted in the late 1950s, increased the mobility of American society and transformed the nation's landscape. It also gave plentiful resources to power brokers to destroy urban neighborhoods, and to disperse people and jobs to the crabgrass frontier of the suburbs.[129]

How the state and local governments invest in public infrastructure systems today will determine how well society functions in the future.[130] This is not a trivial responsibility. Strategic investments will shape the future. Public sector investments in core systems such as water and sewer are essential to maintain and improve community quality of life. Investments in highway and transit systems are essential because mobility is an important aspect of quality of life.

Governor Roy Barnes convinced the Georgia legislature in 1999 to create a strong transportation authority for the Atlanta region to ease congestion and guide development. Maryland Governor Parris

Glendening and New Jersey Governor Christine Todd Whitman have had some success in guiding development to town centers and areas that have the capacity to accommodate additional growth. Governor Tom Ridge of Pennsylvania has also articulated clear land use objectives to guide future growth.[131] Some of the western governors have also been leaders in applying "smart growth" techniques to guide future land use development.[132]

Telecommunications infrastructure investment by the incumbent providers and new entrants may be the most significant investment decision that public sector leaders can influence. This infrastructure may have the same effect in determining the economic viability of communities in the 21st century as did the railroads, which gave life to the communities in their path in the 19th century. Most state and local officials understand that the railroads and highways were the arteries of commerce during the industrial revolution, and that the telecommunications infrastructure, carrying packets of bits (the digital 1s and 0s), are the lifelines of the new knowledge economy. Much has been written about the "digital divide," the split between the "information haves" and the "information-havenots."[133]

Of equal significance is the challenge to determine appropriate public sector strategies to encourage private sector infrastructure investment in distinct geographic communities that lack effective demand for advanced telecommunications services: inner-city neighborhoods and rural communities. Governments have traditionally supported the development of network industries—giving federal lands to the railroads, establishing rate structures loaded with cross-subsidies to expand the publicly switched telephone network and keep residential rates low to expand access to these services, and financing the National Defense Interstate Highway system.[134] Since the enactment of the Telecommunications Act of 1996, future investment decisions will be driven primarily by market criteria; huge investments are being made in urban and suburban communities because that is where firms are confident the future demand for advanced telecommunications services will be sufficiently robust. Investment in inner-city neighborhoods and rural communities may lag because future demand for these services is unproven. Hence, developing a variety of effective strategies to encourage infrastructure investment in these areas may constitute a new burden on the public sector.[135]

The Connecting Minnesota initiative is one pragmatic approach to achieve this important goal that merits attention. The state traded the right-of-way access along its highways to providers who will install and maintain fiber optic cables; some of the new capacity will reserved for state and local government use. Below is a summary (also visit: www.dot.state.mn.us/projects/fiber/index.shtml):

> Under the initiative, Minnesota granted right-of-way access along 2,000 miles of Interstate highway to International Communications Services (ICS) and Universal Communication Networks (UCN). ICS and UCN will install fiber optic technology alongside the roads, with state and local agencies receiving 20 percent of the capacity. ICS and UCN will lease the remaining 80 percent to telecommunications providers and maintain the $195 million network backbone.[136]

Goal #4: To Reshape the State Economic Environment

This set of strategies proposes redesigning economic development programs to match the New Knowledge Economy. The goal of economic development is to create wealth. Economic development is a process, not a product. The development process creates winners and losers. In addition, many are threatened by change. "A successful development strategy must include not only the right policies but also ways of resolving or reducing the economic and political conflicts inherent in the policy making process," advise development experts.[137]

Most of what the states and cities spend on economic development activities is industrial retention and recruitment—another policy legacy from the industrial era.[138] For a variety of institutional and political reasons, jurisdictions will not drop it from their economic development arsenal. Even if industrial recruitment remains as a prominent activity, it should not prevent economic development agencies from redesigning other programs to assist entrepreneurs and small businesses. Governor Tom Ridge of Pennsylvania understands the new approach to economic development is not based on industrial recruitment and tax incentives, but on attracting talent and promoting networking. He observed, "Before the Internet, companies had to find allies where they arose naturally. It used to be 'location, location, location.' Now I think it's more 'network, network, network.' And we can network from any location."[139]

The new knowledge economy celebrates innovation, entrepreneurship, and *"the application of knowledge to work,"* in Peter Drucker's famous phrasing. This means states and cities should be much more active in assisting, promoting, and cultivating entrepreneurs and innovation wherever it occurs. Some jurisdictions do a better job in providing a nurturing business environment than others.

Create and apply knowledge to work

American higher education is the best in the world. Our colleges and universities attract a flood of young people from all over the globe. A rising share of engineering students have foreign visas. (According to Lewis, "By 1996 nearly half of the 55,000 temporary visas issued by the U.S. government to the high-tech workers went to Indians. The definitive smell in a Silicon Valley start-up was of curry."[140]) After graduating, many stay here to work, begin families, and join our society. The lure of American opportunity has become a national competitive advantage.

Can states make better use of their colleges and universities to promote economic development? This strategy is as old as the hills. Enacted in 1862, the Morrill Act established the land-grant universities. Their mission was to develop the "agricultural and mechanic arts." For the next century, they were the dominant institutions in providing applied research to develop natural resources and strengthen state economies. U.S. agriculture became the most productive in the world because farmers substituted capital for labor, used new hybrid seeds and fertilizers, learned crop rotation, and applied new knowledge to every part of their production processes. The role of land-grant universities in developing these improvements can not be overstated. "The investment in agricultural research that produced hybrid corn generated benefits that were about seven times larger than the costs."[141] Indeed, the Agriculture Extension service, a joint federal-state partnership, was instrumental in educating farmers about these innovations. Academics refer to this as the diffusion of innovation.[142]

State universities are tightly bound, by ritual and tradition. They have three social functions: the generation of new knowledge, the teaching of knowledge; and an archive of knowledge. Many have engaged in activities that promote economic development in their states without sacrificing their primary mission. Several have technology transfer programs for small and medium sized manufacturers.[143] They could, in theory, do much more.[144] Business professors could teach marketing to eager entrepreneurs, scientists could collaborate on corporate research and development projects, and computer experts could assist local firms.[145]

> **Social Benefits from Public R & D Investments**
>
> DARPA's expenditure on computer research from the mid-sixties to the mid-eighties amounted to some one billion of (today's) dollars. It was directed at MIT, Stanford, CMU and few other organizations and resulted in generating half the innovations in computer science and technology.
>
> Today, the industrial world economic activity in information technology, made possible by these and other pioneering innovations, is $1.8 trillion a year. Consequently, the return on investment on that early billion dollars from the public purse is around 100,000 percent. I'm sure you'll agree we don't see such ROIs [returns on investment] often.
>
> **Source:** Michael L. Dertouzos, Director, MIT Lab for Computer Science, letter to editor, *Upside*, September 1999.

Here is an example of breaking the traditional mold: A department chair at the University of North Carolina has been given enough flexibility to form his own consulting firm and work part-time with a new startup venture. How could he do this? UNC valued his contributions as a teacher, scholar, and researcher. The university leadership understood that his work away from school was important to his academic responsibilities. It reduced his teaching schedule and administrative duties so he could wear multiple hats. He is gifted and his students will benefit from his outside contacts. The university will not suffer from this flexible arrangement. Yet, few state universities are as flexible as UNC.

In this policy debate, some might ask whether the government should invest in basic science or applied research? That is a false dichotomy. Governments should in invest in both activities. Both kinds of work—abstract science and applied research—"are more productive when they rub up against each other."[146]

Governor John Engler of Michigan in July 1999 announced that his state will devote $50 million a year (from the Tobacco settlement funds) to support research in life science studies. This public investment, about $1 billion over twenty years, will support a cluster of biomedical research institutions and programs in the southern section of Michigan. Governor Engler said, "We wanted to have Michigan well positioned for the future." The combined public and private investment will "assure that Michigan is on the leading edge of biomedical research in the United States and the world."[147]

> **To create an intellectual environment**
>
> "I remember taking economics. . . . There were three factors of production: land, labor and capital. Well, there's a fourth now: ideas, intellect. If you take a look at Nasdaq, right now the marketplace gives ideas even more value as we move into the 21" century than it does land, labor and capital. So there are now four factors of production, *one of the things the government can do is help create the environment where the academic world and the existing technology world expand their environment.*" -- Pennsylvania Governor Tom Ridge (emphasis added).
>
> Source: Interview by Galen Gruman, "A Governor's Tech Crusade," *Upside*, February 2000, 129.

A cynic might contend that most biomedical research is done on the East and West Coasts, there is no way to estimate the social benefits it will generate over two decades, and some of them will flow over the state boundaries. That cynic is wrong. One would have to search long and hard to find a more prudent investment by any state than this one by Michigan, as scientists unlock the mysteries of the double helix and the baby boomer cohort (76 million) begins to dream wistfully of its healthy post-retirement decades ahead. (The first boomer will retire in 2011.) Biotechnology—the integration of microbiology, genetics, molecular biology, biochemistry, and chemical engineering—is emerging as the next "hot" industry, which has the potential to transform modern society far more in the coming decade than the IT sector.[148]

The most successful firms in the 1990s have learned the value of investing in research and development, and applying new knowledge to stay competitive. It is a lesson the states must learn as well. States need to exploit the intellectual assets of its institutions of higher education without subverting their primary social missions.

Foster an Entrepreneurial Culture and Cultivate Venture Capital Formation

The Wall Street Journal reported a study comparing the entrepreneurial experiences of North Americans and Europeans. The researchers concluded that 8.5 percent of U.S. adults would start a business at some point in their lives. The rates for others: 6.8 percent, Canadians; 3.4 percent, Italians; 3.3 percent, Britons; 2.2 percent, Germans; 2 percent, Danes; 1.8 percent, the French; and 1.4 percent of the Finns. Most Germans have a high regard for people involved in business, unlike the Britons, but they remain the most risk-adverse about starting their own businesses.[149] Positive attitudes toward entrepreneurship is an important start, but most states and cities should undertake a sweeping reform in their policies toward small business, including the areas of taxation, business licensing procedures, competitive bidding practices, and public regulation.

Entrepreneurs—who cultivate their dreams, envision new products and services, see market opportunities where corporate executives do not, and create value through persistence and personal drive—contribute to social progress in untold ways. Since most fail, few achieve substantial personal wealth. Yet, they toil and they trouble—sustaining themselves for months at a time on Fritos and pizza and sleeping three hours a night.

Entrepreneurs should be encouraged by the public sector. The road blocks that frustrate small business should be taken down. Taxi driving and hair cuts are commonly held skills, yet public regulation prevents people from providing these basic services. An African-American women in Sacramento was fined by the State of California because she fashioned hair into *cornrows* as a part-time business in her home. Twelve states have laws that protect funeral directors from competition by requiring licenses to sell funeral merchandise. One state requires anyone who wants to sell a casket to the public to first take two years of courses (at a cost of $8,000) and pass an exam on how to embalm a body.[150] Public regulation that unfairly restricts entrepreneurial opportunity does not serve the public interest.

The states have a long tradition of regulating banks, insurance, telecommunication, and electric utilities. Consumer protection remains very important in these essential industries because competitive entry by new providers will invite confusion, chaos, and turbulence. Slamming, the unauthorized switching of long-distance providers, has been one byproduct of the 1996 Telecommunications Act, which partly deregulated telephone services. Other unscrupulous business practices will follow in these industries as a result of deregulation, consolidation, and the rush of new entrants into formally restricted markets. But consumer protection efforts should not be used to restrict entry by qualified entrepreneurs.

State economic development agencies could provide funding to community organizations that provide direct services and technical assistance to potential entrepreneurs. The best source of valuable information on this topic is *State Entrepreneurship Policies and Programs* by Jay Kayne of the Kauffman Center for Entrepreneurial Leadership; available at <www.entreworld.org>.[151] SCORE, an association of retired business people, provides assistance in writing a business plan, designing a marketing study, and establishing an accounting system. Educators have had surprising success in designing entrepreneurship programs in high school settings—students during the day and adults in the evening. Governors can get monthly awards to small business leaders in recognition for their civic contributions, or annual awards to entrepreneurs who create the most new jobs through their growing businesses. Pennsylvania has established a web site where entrepreneurs can find all the government forms they need to start a business. Visit <www.PaOpen4Business.state.pa.us>.

Enter America's companion secret weapon in the New Economy: the venture capitalists. "Venture investments soared to $48.2 billion in 1999 from $19.3 billion the prior year, according to the National Venture Capital Association," reported the *Wall Street Journal*.[152] New startups frequently need additional capital for expansion. If the venture looks promising, outside investors provide the needed capital investment and obtain equity. Advancing the money in exchange for equity in an infant company that has never earned any profits and may never be worth anything is high risk. Most venture-backed companies do not succeed. The few successful ones enter the equity market and both the entrepreneurs and the investors are rewarded for their hard work and good judgment.

One study estimated that Massachusetts alone had as much venture capital as all of Europe, and twenty percent of the European venture funds was invested in the states. Almost every state has a high risk investment program. Some are managed by state agencies. Others are managed by a private firm under contract.[153] Some community development organizations have begun venture capital programs and have formed an association: the Community Development Venture Capital Alliance (<www.cdvca.org>).

The best venture capital programs—both private and public—provide technical assistance and managerial advice to these startup firms, which is often more valuable than the investment. These venture capitalists function as brokers for the small company, enlisting seasoned managerial talent, assisting with business strategy, and opening new doors to potential suppliers and customers. A promising startup in Portland, OR was encouraged to relocate to Silicon Valley after receiving financial support because the investors wanted to keep a watchful eye on, and offer frequent advice to, this promising enterprise. These intangible services are not easy to replicate by those who lack industry expertise and exhaustive Rolodexes. Yet, it serves as an extremely important example of the power of social networking in emerging industries.

Governors, county executives, and mayors should look carefully at the performance of the existing public venture capital programs. Success is not defined by their size, or by the number of investments, but how often these funds and other assistance can nurture entrepreneurial startups so that they achieve a sustainable scale of operations and access to the equity markets. Public sector leaders should also cultivate private venture capitalists to become active in their states and communities.

Nurture Clusters and Facilitate Business Networks

The work of Michael Porter, a professor at the Harvard Business School, provides the intellectual argument for crafting a new wave of economic development strategies. According to Porter,

> The competition among locations has shifted from *comparative advantage* to the broader notion of *competitive advantage*. Comparative advantage due to lower factor costs (for example, labor, raw materials, capital, or infrastructure) or size still exists, but it no longer confers competi-

tive advantage in most industries nor supports high wages. Globalization now allows firms to match comparative advantages by sourcing inputs such as raw materials, capital, and even generic scientific knowledge from anywhere and to disperse selective activities overseas to take advantage of low-cost labor or capital.[154]

Porter contends that traditional locational advantages can not be assumed. Public sector leaders must look very closely at the economic clusters of the firms and suppliers of a region to determine the competitive advantage of a particular location.[155] The state strategic economic development policy should follow the analytical process of searching for value creation and linkages among economic actors in the jurisdiction.[156] A first rate application of this concept has been the design of public-private ventures to design employment training programs—state and local governments working closely with industrial associations to design and manage training programs for the jobs of the future.

Building Competitive Advantage

Access to labor, capital, and natural resources does not determine prosperity, because these have become widely accessible. Rather, competitiveness arises from the productivity with which firms in a location can use inputs to produce valuable goods and services. Moreover, the productivity and prosperity possible in a given location depend not on what industries its firms compete in, but on how they compete. Traditional distinctions between high tech and low tech, or between manufacturing and services, have little relevance in an economy in which virtually all industries can employ advanced technologies and high skill levels to achieve high levels of productivity.

Source: Michael Porter, *On Competition*, 7.

In the mid-1980s, America's two centers for computing innovation were California's Silicon Valley and Massachusetts' Route 128. The general public heard a good deal about the "Massachusetts Miracle" when Governor Dukakis ran for president in 1988, but not much afterward. For good reason, the Massachusetts economy collapsed, and many of the prominent mini-computer companies suffered hard times. Annalee Saxenian's penetrating case study of these two regions provides important lessons about organizational structure and regional advantage in the New Economy.

On the organizational question, Saxenian observes: "Corporations that invested in dedicated equipment and specialized worker skills find themselves locked in to obsolete technologies and markets, while hierarchical structures limit their ability to adapt quickly as conditions change." That was the bad news for the independent firms of Route 128, which "failed to make the transition to smaller workstations and personal computers...." Saxenian thinks the lean, mean, flexible, networked organizational style in Silicon Valley enabled that region to "adapt continuously to fast-changing markets and technologies." Her conclusion about regional advantage must be understood by those forming the next wave of state economic development policy:

> Silicon Valley's network-based system supported a decentralized process of experimentation and learning that fostered successful adaptation, while Route 128's firm-based system was constrained by the isolation of its producers from external sources of know-how and information. Route 128 firms continued to generate technological breakthroughs but were not part of an industrial system that would have enabled them to exploit these successes as a region. In Silicon Valley, as in comparable localities elsewhere, *regional networks promote the collective technological advance that is increasingly essential to competitive success.*[157] (Emphasis added)

Stanford University was a major force in the development of the semiconductor industry in northern California, long before it became known as Silicon Valley. During the same era, North Carolina's public leadership was visionary in promoting its Research Triangle. More recently, New York City helped renovate a downtown building with primitive office space to recruit Web-based startup companies. It fixed up the building and installed advanced telecommunications infrastructure (bandwidth). Using the business incubator approach, it was selective about which companies could rent in this building. It hoped that locating similar firms would create positive synergies among them. This strategy appears to have worked; some refer now to the surrounding neighborhood as Silicon Alley.

Clusters and the New Economics of Competition

Now that companies can source capital, goods, information, and technology from around the world, often with a click of a mouse, much of the conventional wisdom about how companies and nations compete needs to be overhauled. In theory, more open global markets and faster communication should diminish the role of location in competition....

Today's economic map of the world is dominated by what I call *clusters*: critical masses— in one place— of unusual competitive success in particular fields. Clusters are a striking feature of virtually every national, regional, state, and even metropolitan economy, especially in more economically advanced nations. Silicon Valley and Hollywood may be the world's best-known clusters. Clusters are not unique; however; they are highly typical— and therein lies the paradox: the enduring competitive advantages in a global economy lie increasingly in local things— knowledge, relationships, motivation— that distant rivals cannot match.

Source: Michael M. Porter, "Clusters and the New Economics of Competition," *Harvard Business Review*, November- December 1998, 77-8.

The idea of informal networks among firms in an industry, often called a cluster, is not unique to high-tech industries. Examples include the industrial network in northern Italy (Terza Italia), precision metal fabricators in the Piedmont region of North Carolina (which formed an industry association to collaborate with a college for specialized training programs), the 200 firms in the carpet industry near Dalton, GA, the 250 furniture manufacturers near Tupelo, MS, plastics companies in El Paso, TX and southern New England, eyelet manufacturers in Waterbury, CT, machine tool companies in western Pennsylvania, the jewelry makers in Rhode Island, the many secondary wood products firms that participate in the Oregon Wood Product Competitiveness Corporation, and the movie industry in southern California.

Michael Porter uses the California wine cluster to illustrate the range of participants: growers, wineries, suppliers, publicists, academic institutions that provide applied research, and government agencies:

> The California wine cluster...includes 680 commercial wineries as well as several thousand independent wine grape growers....suppliers of grape stock, irrigation and harvesting equipment, barrels, and labels; specialized public relations and advertising firms; and numerous wine publications....A host of local institutions is involved with wine, such as the world-renowned viticulture and enology program at the University of California at Davis, the Wine Institute, and special committees of the California senate and assembly. The cluster also enjoys weaker linkages to other California clusters in agriculture, food, and restaurants, and wine-country tourism.[158]

State economic development agencies understand this theory of industry clusters and vary in the range of support provided to them. Often this process begins with a survey of the state or regional economy. Its strengths and weaknesses are identified. Then a public-private partnership is formed to direct activities such as researching market trends, reforming antiquated regulations, or developing a common export strategy.[159]

The strongest claims that using a sector approach has successfully targeted high-tech firms have been made by officials in Arizona, Virginia, and Oregon. Janet Jones, who ran Oregon's project, said, "The whole idea was to focus on high-tech and get off the over-dependence on forest products." According to Jones, the number of high-tech jobs grew from 35,000 in 1980 to 72,000 in 1998. During the same period, the state lost 20,000 lumber jobs. Jones observed, "Oregon now has so many high tech jobs, the emphasis has shifted from recruitment to assisting the companies right here, and working with communities to manage their development."[160]

Economic development agencies can assist industry leaders in organizing industry associations to pursue common goals. A frequent task of industry associations is to negotiate with community colleges to provide appropriate training for their employees. Joint training programs also provide informal opportunities for employees of different firms to learn from each other. The paramount objective is to encourage firms to communicate and learn from each other. Silicon Valley firms value, Saxenian observed, "Social relationships and even gossip as a crucial aspect of their businesses. In an industry characterized by rapid technological change and intense competition, informal communication was often of more value than more conventional but less timely forums such as industry journals."[161]

Successful firms learn about innovation from within their organizations and from outside them. As Michael Best emphasizes in *The New Competition*, "For a learning firm, improvement is always possible and ideas for improvement can come from everyone, including customers, workers, suppliers, staff, and managers. As a social process, innovation involves the interaction of people engaged in functionally distinct activities."[162] Social networking among firms in a cluster of industries can be encouraged and assisted by the public sector.

Reform the Tax Structure

Interjurisdictional tax competition has accelerated in recent years. More firms are threatening to leave their existing locations unless they obtain specific tax concessions. On the other hand, the recruitment of business investment among jurisdictions has become very competitive. Mercedes-Benz considered more than 100 sites in thirty-five states prior to selecting the Alabama location in 1993.

> **Globalization Complicates Taxation of Capital and Income**
>
> Globalization is a tax problem for three reasons. First, firms have more freedom over where to locate. Activities that require only a screen, a telephone and a modem can be located anywhere. This will make it harder for a country to tax businesses more heavily than its competitors....
> Second, globalization makes it hard to decide where a company should pay taxes, regardless of where it is based. Multinational firms design their product in one country, manufacture in another, and sell in a third. This gives them plenty of scope to reduce tax bills by shifting operations around or by crafty transfer-pricing....
> The third reason why globalization is a problem is that...it nibbles away at the edges of taxes on individuals. It is harder to tax personal income, because skilled professional workers are more mobile than they were two decades ago. Even if they do not become tax exiles, many earn a growing slice of their income from overseas....Such income is relatively easy to hide from the taxman.
>
> **Source:** "Disappearing Taxes," *The Economist*, May 31, 1997, 21.

These two trends reflect the same phenomenon—capital is mobile. Walter Wriston, former Citibank chair, observed, "Money flows to what it is wanted and stays where it is well-treated." The mobility of capital makes it difficult to tax, a problem that will grow more difficult in the digital future. As the nature of work changes in the future, a growing share of jobs will be portable, no longer place-specific.

One pragmatic response to the problem of the interjurisdictional tax competition is to lower tax rates to match that of neighboring states. Ultimately, this path leads to the erosion of the tax base and shifting the tax burden onto other revenue sources, which further distorts economic behavior and discourages other private investment. The demand for quality public services, however, increases with population growth and as society gains affluence. State sovereignty and municipal independence are linked to their respective abilities to respond to the demands and needs of the public.

When the current state-local tax structure was constructed in the 1930s, most local and regional economies were tightly bound to geography. In that industrial era, most people worked, shopped, and lived in the same community. In these "closed" systems, jurisdictions had a relatively easy time taxing income and consumption to raise sufficient revenue to support public services. The global economy today is an open system of economic production and consumption. The major vulnerability of the current state-local tax structure is its inability to adapt to increased mobility.

A 1998 report published by the National League of Cities (co-sponsored by NGA and NCSL) made similar assessments:

1. The traditional state-local tax structure lags behind the economic transformation of the information age. For example, states generally tax tangible goods but not

services—a growing sector of the economy. Public sector revenues from the sales tax—about one-quarter of all state-local tax revenues—could be subverted by the growth of electronic commerce.

2. The national and state deregulation of telecommunications and electric industries will force state and local tax reform. Liberalizing these markets will trigger the end of discriminatory taxes, the legacy of the regulated monopoly era.

3. The demographic shifts projected in the coming decade or two, as America ages, will constrain public sector revenues and impose huge demands for social services.

4. The digital convergence of computing and communications has changed the nature of work and the ease of shifting it to competing locations.

5. Increased global competition and capital mobility facilitate the dispersal of production facilities throughout the world and heighten tax competition among jurisdictions. And,

6. In the context of these multiple pressures, the future autonomy of state and local governments may rest on their ability to generate sufficient revenues to provide quality services and maximize their locational advantages.[163]

Tax reformers provide three general recommendations: a tax structure should provide sufficient revenues to enable elected officials to exercise discretion and autonomy in responding to public needs; a range of taxes may be superior to relying heavily upon a few sources (each tax is imperfect in its own way); and taxes with low rates and a broad base minimize economic distortions.

> ### NGA Policy on Expanded Duty to Collect and Simplification of State Sales-Use Taxes
>
> The Governors have called for the development of a twenty-first century sales tax that can achieve fairness for all forms of sales: Main Street, mail order, and Internet. A streamlined sales tax with simplified compliance requirements will ensure that states are prepared to support the global electronic marketplace of the next century.
>
> **Source:** EC-12 Streamlining State Sales Tax Systems, NGA Policy, Adopted Winter Meeting 1999.

These public finance principles may help the governors respond to two pressing tax controversies:

1. Reforming discriminatory telecommunications taxes on wireline providers, an historical legacy from the monopoly provider era, which can not be sustained in a competitive environment. [164] How can tax equity be achieved in a way that is technologically neutral? In the digital future, all communications will be data (the digital bits of 1s and 0s transmitted in packets) sent in countless ways: wireline, wireless, coax-cable, fiber optics, HDTV, satellite, Internet, and so on. Why should tax policy bear so heavily upon wireline providers while other providers using new technologies and different modes are lightly taxed? Which telecommunications services should be taxed? And, by which level of government?[165]

2. Redefining nexus to govern remote commerce. Expanding the duty by remote vendors to collect the sales/use tax and simplifying various state tax laws is a superior approach to the present stalemate, but it will require the collective effort of the governors to negotiate with the private sector and to educate Congress.[166] At the first meeting of Advisory Commission on Electronic Commerce in June 1999, Utah Governor Michael Leavitt said, "There is a time that every problem is big enough that you see it, but small enough that you can solve it. This is the time and this is that problem."

As we enter the digital age, the prospect of accelerating growth in retail electronic commerce may be the most visible long-term threat to the existing state-local tax structure. The Department of Commerce estimates $5.3 billion in online sales by retail establishments in the fourth quarter of 1999.[167] Forrester Research estimated that 17 million Americans in 1999 spent $20 billion on goods electronically. "Both of those figures are widely expected to grow sharply this year," writes a reporter from the *Wall Street Journal*.[168] Two public finance experts at the University of Tennessee estimate retail e-commerce "will cause about $10.8 billion in additional tax revenue losses nationwide in 2003."[169] (For more on this topic, see Appendix A and B.)

The advent of electronic commerce liberates consumption from geography and heightens capital mobility. The mobility of firms forces interjurisdictional tax competition, and makes it more difficult to tax income and capital. State governments today collect a much smaller share of its revenue from business than in past decades.[170] What is a rational basis for taxing business so that it also contributes to the public sector to support public services?[171]

The new era of allowing competitive entry in telecommunications and electric industries poses an extraordinary challenge to the states in reforming past discriminatory taxes on these previously regulated industries. On the horizon, the aging of

America will shift relative tax burdens among age cohorts. The growing elderly population will likely consume less than the working age population and spend a larger share of their incomes on services, such as health care, which are often not taxed. In addition, the controversy over granting a full array of senior tax preferences will escalate in the coming decade as the demographic shift becomes more pronounced and the champions of generational equity gain more support among the working age population. Taken together, these economic, social, demographic, and technological trends threaten to imperil the future viability of the state-local tax structure. Governors must work closely with state legislative leaders and with Congress to confront these challenges. Failing to do so soon could undermine the viability of the state-local tax structure in the years ahead, jeopardizing state autonomy.[172]

The best time for comprehensive tax reform is when the states have sufficient revenues. More than four of five states have budget surpluses. The rosy glow from having a flush treasury, unfortunately, leads to inertia and complacency. "If it ain't broke, don't fix it," Bert Lance used to say. The state-local tax structure needs corrective surgery. The time to do this is now, while the patient is healthy. Anyone who has served as a state legislator, member of the city council, or as a county executive during a recession can testify to the painful choices that must be made. Angry constituents who protest proposed cuts in valuable public services are matched by equally angry constituents who oppose tax increases to plug the gap in the budget. Political expediency, a cruel master, guides those most unpleasant choices. That will be the least likely time in which to reform the state-local tax structure to minimize its economic distortions, attract investment, promote economic development, and achieve tax neutrality. This is the time to act—the time to heed Aaron Wildavsky's advice, "It is up to the wise to undo the damage done by the merely good."[173]

Strategies to create a hospitable environment for the 21st century economy:

Sustaining public investments in applied programs at the state university and colleges in agriculture, forestry, mining, and other areas of natural resource development. Similar manufacturing extension programs for small and medium size firms have demonstrated much promise. Michigan has chosen the biomedical sciences as a strategic investment for public research and development.

Encouraging faculty at public institutions to work with industry associations to develop expertise that can be broadly distributed to budding entrepreneurs and small business managers.

Streamlining the regulatory and tax systems to eliminate unnecessary burdens on entrepreneurs and small business operators.

Developing mentoring programs to assist entrepreneurs and the leaders of small firms.

Forming public-private partnerships to promote venture capital formation and create business networks. And

Reforming the State-Local Tax Structure.

ADAPTING TO CHANGE TO ENHANCE FUTURE PROSPERITY

Economic history is littered with examples of how governments have made distinct policy choices, resulting in jarringly different outcomes. Paul Romer has compared Britain and the United States from 1870 to 1994. In 1870, Britain was the worldwide leader in technology and had the highest standard of living in the world—its per capita income was 1.3 greater than that of the U.S. Its leadership was clearly dominant at the early stage of the industrial revolution. Over the next 124 years, Britain's per capita income level increased at a rate just one half of a percentage point below the U.S. growth rate. In 1994, Britain's per capita income was only 0.72 times as large as the U.S. per capita income level. In dollar terms, the U.S. income per person was about $6,000 higher than it was in Britain in 1994.[174]

This comparison draws attention to a several of America's advantages (even though Britain had first-mover advantages in the industrial revolution): 1. A society open to people from other lands and new ideas; 2. An entrepreneurial culture that rewarded initiative and celebrated success; 3. Public policies that expanded educational and employment opportunities broadly; 4. Public sector investment in both abstract science and applied research. And 5. An ability of the public sector to change how it performed the business of government. These lessons can be applied today to respond to the new economy.

States have had a long history of developing innovative economic development policies. Usually a few states were the first to adapt to changing circumstances, followed by the others. When natural resources were the primary source of wealth, the states built canals and railroads to get those goods to market; they also supported research and development at universities to learn how to make the best use of their natural resources to advance their economies. In the late 19th century, when the industrial revolution began to heat up, the states chartered corporations, supported entrepreneurial capitalism, and the tolerated industrial titans who organized giant industries such as steel production, oil refining, and vast webs of railroads. Early in the twentieth century, when the mass assembly lines of Henry Ford and others required skilled workers, the states imposed high school attendance requirements and established educational institutions to serve that growing industrial need.

Now that knowledge has become the most important factor of production, the public sector's role in facilitating the creation of social wealth must be understood. The first movers will capture competitive advantage. Technology is advancing at lightning speed. Public policy is often formed in a democratic society at a crawl. Only the leadership of the governors and mayors can change the organizational cultures of their governments quickly enough to capture the full benefits of the New Economy. Sun Microsystems CEO Scott McNealy spoke about the Internet: "It's equal opportunity if you're online. But," McNealy warned, "if you're not, it isn't."[175] State and local governments have "to get with it" and "get on it."

This New Knowledge Economy represents an array of management challenges to elected officials and public sector managers: how to push state and local governments to adapt to these external forces, transform how public sector work can be done, experiment with new approaches, and develop new strategies for responding to age-old problems? Can the states and cities adapt to the economic transformation from goods-production to services, from materials-based to knowledge-intensive activities, from analogue to digital, from old to new? Will some public leaders be more strategic than their counterparts in making public investments, improving public education, adapting training programs for adult workers to prepare them for the jobs of the future, and forming public-private partnerships to guide the next wave of economic development activities?

Some leaders are beginning to adapt to this New Knowledge Economy and their jurisdictions—earning the *first mover* advantage—will be in the best position to enjoy future prosperity. Firms, knowledge workers, entrepreneurs and direct foreign investment will flow to them like iron filings to a magnet.

Pennsylvania Governor Tom Ridge believes that promoting social networking is a promising growth strategies, and civil leaders in Pittsburgh understand that amenities and quality of life enhancements are necessary to attract talented workers. Governor Gray Davis wants the California state government to provide services 24-7, and Maine Governor Angus King proposed that a free laptop computer be given to every seventh grader. Governor John Engler has invested much of the Tobacco settlement funds in Michigan's intellectual infrastructure to nurture biomedical research at the state universities. Governor Parris Glendening has been a strong leader in advocating "smart growth" techniques to improve the quality of life in Maryland, and Georgia Governor Roy Barnes is trying to ease traffic congestion in the Atlanta metropolitan region. Governor George Ryan made transportation infrastructure investment one of his top priorities in his first year of office; his initiative, called Illinois First, invests $12 billion over five years into improving roads, subways, high-speed rail, and school construction.[176]

Some of the other states, frozen in their own inertia, will fail to adapt to this New Knowledge Economy, or fail to move very quickly and will fall behind. The laggards are much less likely to enjoy increasing prosperity. State economies in the 21st century dependent upon natural resource development and mass production will remain well below the national average in terms of income, job growth, and private investment. Those states, wallowing in their own complacency, may fail to foster innovation and entrepreneurship, may fail to prepare youth and adults for future jobs, may fail to attract venture capital, and may fail to form effective public-private partnerships. If so, they will fail to adapt to this transition to the New Economy, just as surely as the dinosaurs failed to cope with the climate change of the last Ice Age.

States and cities need 21st century strategies to enhance the value of place as the forces of the digital revolution and the integrated global economy transcend geographic boundaries. They need new approaches to promote life-long learning because the skills required for jobs in the 21st century economy will be steadily rising, job churning higher than it is today, and knowledge has become the dominant factor of production.

The New Role of Government

Nothing, said Victor Hugo, is as powerful as an idea whose time has come. Government's first mission is to create an environment that encourages those new ideas. Reinvention is not possible without new ideas. But continuous reinvention will ultimately not work just because of the excellence of the ideas, but also because citizens themselves are involved in coming up with those ideas.

Source: Blake Harris, "Empowering the Digital Citizen," Special Issue, *Government Technology*, August 1999, 47.

State and local officials can learn much from leading service sector firms about benchmarking, performance-based measures and accountability, and how to best use purchasing, privatization, and markets to achieve social outcomes. The organizational culture of these governments must be changed to put customer service first. Citizens in the 21st century will require "high tech and high touch" services from the public sector.

State and local governments also need a fresh approach to economic development that eases burdens on small businesses, assists entrepreneurs, cultivates venture capital formation, and rewards innovation wherever it might take seed. Amenities and quality of life will attract the knowledge workers of the future to our communities. Elected officials who invest strategically to enhance the value of place and employ new governance strategies will enjoy increased prosperity in their communities. Competing in the New Knowledge Economy will require all this and more.

ENDNOTES

[1] For the first interpretation, see Raymond Vernon, *Sovereignty at Bay: The Multinational Spread of U.S. Enterprises* (New York: Basic Books, 1971); Robert Kuttner, *Everything For Sale: The Virtues and Limits of Markets* (NY: Knopf, 1998) and Daniel Yergin and Joseph Stanislaw, *The Commanding Heights: The Battle Between Government and the Marketplace That Is Remaking the Modern World* (New York: Simon & Schuster, 1998). For the second interpretation, see James R. Beniger, *The Control Revolution: Technological and Economic Origins of the Information Society* (Cambridge, MA: Harvard University Press, 1986); Walter Wriston, *The Twilight of Sovereignty: How the Information Revolution is Transforming Our World* (New York: Charles Scribner's Sons, 1992); and Andrew L. Shapiro, *The Control Revolution: How the Internet is Putting Individuals in Charge and Changing the World We Know* (New York: PublicAffairs, 1999).

As evidence of the decline of sovereignty, taxation in the New Economy is clearly the biggest challenge facing governments. One example comes from the corporate use of "transfer pricing," the accounting technique that allocations corporate income to various locations. Some critics allege that transfer pricing, by attributing more income to low-tax jurisdictions, is used to reduce corporate tax liability. Tax avoidance is legal; tax evasion is not. An embarrassing consequence of this practice is called "phantom states." This happens when corporations report more income to the federal government than the sum of what is allocated among the states where they conduct business. For a discussion of this issue, see Dan R. Bucks and Michael Mazerov, "The State Solution to the Federal Government's International Transfer Pricing Problem," *National Tax Journal*

Volume XLVI, no. 3 (September 1993). For the larger issue of how corporations have become inventive in their allocation of income across various jurisdictions, see Richard D. Pomp, "The Future of the State Corporate Income Tax: Reflections (and Confessions) of a Tax Lawyer," David Brunori, editor, *The Future of State Taxation* (Washington, D.C.: Urban Institute Press, 1998). For a general discussion of the problem of taxation in the New Economy, see Thomas W. Bonnett, *Is the New Global Economy Leaving State-Local Tax Structures Behind?* (Washington, D.C.: National League of Cities, 1998).

Evidence of that control is shifting to consumers from the availability of more information via the Internet comes from Robert Davis and Leslie Miller, "Net Empowering Patients," *USA Today*, July 14, 1999. This article reports that 7.8 million U.S. adults obtained health information from the Internet in 1996; this number had increased to 22 million in 1998, and is projected to be 33 million in 2000. Davis and Miller quote J. Sybil Biermann, a surgeon at the University of Michigan, on how this could affect the doctor-patient relationship: "Every doctor needs to be prepared for the day when someone comes in with more information that we don't know about. We need to be prepared and accept that and learn from our patients. It's a new idea of how things should go in the typical medical model."

[2] Alan M. Webber, "What's So New About the New Economy," *Harvard Business Review*, January-February 1993.

[3] Lestor C. Throw, "Building Wealth, *The Atlantic Monthly*, June 1999, 59.

[4] David R. Henderson, "Honor entrepreneurs," *Red Herring*, July 1999, 152 cites the following passage from Joseph Schumpeter's 1942 classic, *Capitalism, Socialism, and Democracy* to demonstrate that an emphasis on price competition misses the major theme—how competition fosters dynamic changes:

But in capitalist reality as distinguished from its textbook picture, it is not that kind of competition which counts but the competition from the new commodity, the new technology, the new source of supply, the new type of organization . . . competition which commands a decisive cost or quality advantage and which strikes not the margins of profits and the outputs of existing firms but at their foundations and their very lives.

5 Anthony Patrick Carnevale, *America and the New Economy* (Alexandria, VA: American Society for Training and Development, and U.S. Department of Labor, Employment and Training Administration, Washington, D.C., 1991), iii.

6 Webber, "What's So New About the New Economy?" See Don Tapscott, *The Digital Economy: Promise and Peril in the Age of Networked Intelligence* (NY: McGraw-Hill, 1996). In that book and a subsequent book he edited, *Created Value in the Network Economy* (Boston: Harvard Business School Press, 1999), Tapscott responds substantively to Webber's question and with a story about when Albert Einstein was monitoring a graduate school physics exam. According Tapscott, "One student pointed out that the questions on the exam were the same as those on the previous year's test. 'That's okay,' Einstein replied, 'The answers are different this year.'"

7 Brian Winston, *Media Technology and Society—A History: From the Telegraph to the Internet* (NY: Routledge, 1998), 142.

8 See the papers presented at the Conference "Understanding the Digital Economy: Data, Tools and Research," hosted by the U.S. Department of Commerce, Washington, D.C., May 25–26, 1999. Available at [http://www.digitaleconomy.gov].

9 See Testimony of Chairman Alan Greenspan, "High-tech industry in the U.S. economy," before the Joint Economic Committee, United State Congress, June 14, 1999.

10 John Cassidy, "The Experiment," *The New Yorker*, May 24, 1999, 50.

11 An extreme view was summarized in *The Economist* (July 24, 1999), 21: "Computer technology coupled with a global marketplace, they argued, would allow America's economy to grow much faster without overheating. Men of true faith went further: inflation was dead, they claimed, the business cycle was abolished

and the old economic rules repealed." For a range of views, see Alan Goldstein, "Milken panel evaluates impact of technology," *Dallas Morning News*, March 10, 2000; Alan S. Blinder, "The Internet and the New Economy," available at www.brookings.edu/views/papers/blinder; Robert Gordon, "Has the 'New Economy' rendered the productivity slowdown obsolete?" available at http://faculty-web.at.nwu.edu/economics/gordon; and the papers presented at "Understanding the Digital Economy: Data, Tools and Research," U.S. Department of Commerce, Washington, D.C., May 1999.

[12] Edward Chancellor, *Devil Take the Hindmost: A History of Financial Speculation* (NY: Farrar, Straus, Giroux, 1999), 283.

[13] Douglass C. North, *Institutions, Institutional Change and Economic Performance* (NY: Cambridge University Press, 1991), 80.

[14] Dale Neef, "Why Knowledge, Why Now?" Dale Neef, editor, *The Knowledge Economy* (Boston: Butterworth-Heinemann, 1998), 2.

[15] Thomas L. Friedman, *The Lexus and the Olive Tree: Understanding Globalization* (NY: Farrar, Straus, Giroux, 1999), xiv.

[16] This discussion follows the arguments developed in Thomas W. Bonnett, *Governance in the Digital Age* (Washington, D.C.: National League of Cities, 1999); 13–21 and Appendix B.

[17] Daniel Yergin and Joseph Stanislaw, *The Commanding Heights: The Battle Between Governments and the Marketplace that is Remaking the Modern World* (NY: Simon & Schuster, 1998), 195–6.

[18] Webber, "What's So New About the New Economy,", see also Wriston, 1972.

[19] David C. Mowery and Nathan Rosenberg, *Paths of Innovation: Technological Change in the 20th Century America* (NY: Cambridge University Press, 1998), 172–3.

[20] Gary Hufbauer, "World Economic Integration: The Long View," *International Economic Insights*, 11 (May-June 1991).

[21] James Burnham, "The Growing Impact of Global Telecommunications on the Location of Work," Contemporary Issues #87

(Washington University, St. Louis: Center for the Study of American Business, October 1997).

22. As cited in Barry M. Hager, *Limiting Risks and Sharing Losses in the Globalized Capital Market* (Washington, D.C.: Woodrow Wilson Center Press, 1998), 5.

23. Elinor Harris Solomon, *Virtual Money: Understanding the Power and Risks of Money's High-Speed Journey Into Electronic Space* (NY: Oxford University Press, 1997).

24. Robert Reich, *The Work of Nations* (NY: Knopf, 1991), 112.

25. Boris Pleskovic, "Challenges for the New Economic Geography in the Twenty-First Century," *International Regional Science Review* 22, 2:140 (August 1999).

26. See Eamonn Fingleton, *In Praise of Hard Industries: Why Manufacturing, not the Information Economy, is the Key to Future Prosperity* (NY: Houghton Mifflin, 1999).

27. Neef, "Why Knowledge, Why Now?" 3.

28. See Thomas W. Bonnett, *Governance in the Digital Age: The Impact of the Global Economy, Information Technology and Economic Deregulation on State and Local Government* (Washington, D.C.: National League of Cities, 1999), 23.

29. Edward Luttwak, *Turbo-Capitalism: Winners and Losers in the Global Economy* (NY: Harper-Collins, 1999).

30. Lester C. Thurow, *The Future of Capitalism* (NY: William Morrow & Co., Inc., 1996).

31. As cited in Brian Winston, *Media Technology and Society—A History: From the Telegraph to the Internet* (NY: Routledge, 1999), 336.

32. As quoted in Michael Lewis, *The New New Thing* (NY: Norton, 2000), 251.

33. "Gordon Moore, an inventor of the integrated circuit and then chairman of Intel, noted in 1965 that the surface area of a transistor (as etched on an integrated circuit) was being reduced by approximately 50 percent every twelve months. In 1975, he was widely reported to have revised this observation to eighteen months. Moore claims that his 1975 update was to

twenty-four months, and that does appear to be a better fit to the data. The result is that every two years, you can pack twice as many transistors on an integrated circuit. This doubles both the number of components on a chip a well as its speed. Since the cost of an integrated circuit is fairly constant, the implication is that every two years you can get twice as much circuitry running at twice the speed for the same price. For many applications, that's an effective quadrupling of the value. The observation holds true for every type of circuit, from memory chips to computer processors. This insightful observation has become known as Moore's Law on Integrated Circuits, and the remarkable phenomenon of the law has been driving the acceleration of computing for the past forty years." Ray Kurzwell, *The Age of Spiritual Machines* (NY: Penguin Books, 1999), 20–21.

[34] David Henry, Patricia Buckley, Gurmukh Gill, Sandra Cooke, Jess Dumagan, Dennis Pastore, Susan LaPorte, *The Emerging Digital Economy II* (Washington, D.C.: Secretariat on Electronic Commerce, U.S. Department of Commerce, June 1999), Executive Summary; see also *Digital Economy 2000*, Economic and Statistics Administration, U.S. Department of Commerce, (available at http://www/esa.doc.gov/de2000.pdf), 27: "IT industries produce less than 10 percent of total U.S. output. Nevertheless, between 1995 and 1999, because of IT industries' extraordinary growth and falling prices, they accounted for an average 30 percent of total real U.S. economic growth."

[35] Hal R. Varian, "Economic Issues Facing the Internet," *The Internet as Paradigm* (Queenstown, MD: Institute for Information Studies, 1997), 28.

[36] This discussion relies heavily upon Robert H. Reid, *Architects of the Web: 1,000 Days That Built the Future of Business*, Chapter 1 (NY: John Wiley & Sons, Inc., 1997).

[37] Lewis, *The New New Thing*, 30.

[38] "Metrics," *The Industry Standard*, March 6, 2000, 174.

[39] Don Tapscott, "Introduction" in *Creating Value in the Network Economy*, xiv.

[40] See, for example, Thomas W. Malone and Robert J. Laubacher, "The Dawn of the E-Lance Economy," in *Creating Value in the Network Economy*.
[41] Geoffrey Colvin, "The Year of the Megamerger," *Fortune*, January 11, 1999.
[42] As quoted in John Cassidy, "The Woman in the Bubble," *The New Yorker*, April 26 & May 3, 1999, 62.
[43] Thurow, *The Future of Capitalism*.
[44] Tapscott, "Introduction," viii.
[45] James F. Moore, *The Death of Competition: Leadership & Strategy in the Age of Business Ecosystems* (NY: HarperBusiness, 1996), 182.
[46] See Chancellor, *Devil Take the Hindmost*; and John Cassidy, "Wall Street Follies," *The New Yorker*, August 9, 1999, 29. Cassidy notes that early in 1999 AOL's stock reached 175, "valuing America Online at north of a hundred and fifty billion dollars, more than Disney and Time Warner combined." He also compares America Online's stock value from 1994 to 1999 with the stock value of the Radio Corp. of America (RCA) from 1924 to 1929, when it peaked.
[47] E. S. Browning, "Deja Vu All Over Again: Nasdaq Passes 4000," *Wall Street Journal*, June 21, 2000, C1.
[48] Thomas L. Friedman, "The Invisible Men," *New York Times*, February 2, 1998, A19.
[49] Ronald H. Coase, "The Nature of the Firm," (1937) reprinted in Oliver E. Williamson and Sidney G. Winter, editors, *The Nature of the Firm* (NY: Oxford University Press, 1993), 25.
[50] Nevin Cohen, "Greening the Internet: Ten Ways E-Commerce Could Affect the Environment," *Environmental Quality Review*, 1999.
[51] Rebecca Smith Hurd, "E-Sales Expected to Soar Amid Consolidation," Techweb News, cmpnet.com, June 27, 2000, (available at http://www.techweb.com/).
[52] Bill Gates with Nathan Myhrvold and Peter Rinearson, *The Road Ahead* (NY: Pengiun, 1996), 181.

[53] "Nearly Half of U.S. Homes Now Have Access to Web," *Wall Street Journal*, June 19, 2000, B18: "Internet users have almost become an American majority, with 49% of U.S. homes online in May. . . . Those online were staying on longer and looking at more pages. The number of pages viewed per month per person rose 21% to 662 pages from 548 pages, while the hours per month rose 9.7% to nine hours and five minutes from eight hours and 17 minutes."

[54] David Henry, et al, *The Emerging Digital Economy II*, (Washington, D.C.: Economics and Statistics Administration, Department of Commerce, June 1999), 4–5.

[55] George Anders, "Some Big Companies Long to Embrace Web But Settle for Flirtation," *Wall Street Journal*, November 4, 1998, 1.

[56] Dertouzos as quoted by Claudia Dreufus, "A Pragmatist on What Computers Can Do," *New York Times*, July 4, 1999, [Gates] "thinks consumers and suppliers are going to meet on this gigantic football field called the Internet and they are going to do deals together without an intermediary. It's a seductive idea.

In my opinion, it is right for about 15 percent of the marketplace. But wrong for 85 percent. It will happen on standard products and products that do not involve trust questions—relatively small products."

[57] Jerry Useem, "Internet Defense Strategy: Cannibalize Yourself," *Fortune*, September 6, 1999.

[58] Bloomberg News, "Study Predicts Hugh Growth in Business-to-Business Web Sector," *New York Times*, June 27, 2000, C6.

[59] Lynn Margherio et al, *The Emerging Digital Economy* (Washington, D.C.: Department of Commerce, April 1998), 14–5.

[60] Thomas L. Friedman, *The Lexus and the Olive Tree: Understanding Globalization* (NY: Farrar, Straus and Giroux, 1999).

[61] *The Economic and Social Impacts of Electronic Commerce: Preliminary Findings and Research Agenda* (Washington, D.C.: OECD, September 1998, 24. For those concerned about the adaptive capacity of society to respond to rapid economic and social changes, it is sobering to reflect on why the wave

of globalization following this inventive era could not be sustained. See Dan Rodrik, "The Debate Over Globalization: How to Move Forward by Looking Backward," Jeffrey J. Schott, editor, *Launching New Global Trade Talks: An Action Agenda* (Washington, D.C.: Institute for International Economics, September 1998). The first half of the 20th century was tragic: two world wars within thirty years and, between them, a global depression that lasted almost a decade.

[62] Robert Pool, *Beyond Engineering: How Society Shapes Technology* (NY: Oxford University Press, 1997).

[63] Brian Winston, *Media Technology and Society—A History: From the Telegraph to the Internet* (NY: Routledge, 1999).

[64] Maurice Estabrooks, *Electronic Technology, Corporate Strategy, and World Transformation* (Westport, CT: Quorum Books, 1995), 173.

[65] Jeff Cole, "Boeing Expects $4.7 Billion in 777 Model Orders," *Wall Street Journal*, June 28, 2000, A2.

[66] Tapscott, "Introduction," xx.

[67] Thurow, *The Future of Capitalism*.

[68] Peter Drucker, *Post-Capitalist Society* (NY: HarperCollins, 1993), 40.

[69] Dale Neef, "Why Knowledge, Why Now?" in *The Knowledge Economy* (Boston: Butterworth-Heinemann, 1998), 2.

[70] Virginia Postrel, "The Work Ethic, Redefined," *Wall Street Journal*, September 4, 1998.

[71] Robert Kuttner, *Everything for Sale: The Virtues and Limits of Markets* (NY: Knopf, 1998), 193.

[72] Edward F. Dension, *Trends in American Economic Growth, 1929–1982* (Washington, D.C.: Brookings Institution, 1985), 44.

[73] See Charles I. Jones, Sources of U.S. Economic Growth in a World of Ideas, unpublished, Department of Economics, Stanford University; available at <www.stanford.edu/~chadj>.

[74] As cited in Earl H. Fry, *The Expanding Role of State and Local Governments in U.S. Foreign Affairs* (NY: Council on Foreign Relations, 1998), n34, 11.

75 As cited in Danny T. Quah, "The Invisible Hand and the Weightless Economy," London School of Economics, mimeo, April 1996.
76 Kurzwell, *The Age of Spiritual Machines*, 101.
77 Lewis, *The New New Thing*, 31.
78 W. Brian Arthur, "Increasing Returns and the New World of Business, *Harvard Business Review*, July-August 1996, 100.
79 Clayton M. Christensen, *The Innovator's Dilemma: When New Technologies Cause Great Firms to Fail* (Boston: Harvard Business School Press, 1997).
80 Carl Shapiro and Hal R. Varian, *Information Rules: A Strategic Guide to the Network Economy* (Boston: Harvard Business School Press, 1999), 224.
81 "Networks, like telephone networks or the Internet, are subject to a phenomenon called 'network effects' or network externalities.' Establishing a network involves large, up-front fixed costs (e.g., for purchasing equipment, laying new cable, or developing new software), but adding an additional user to an existing network costs very little. Conversely, the value of the network to participants is low when the number of participants on the network is low, but rises rapidly as network participation expands. For example, the network of a single telephone is of no use. Adding another telephone increases the value of the network because now calls can be made between the two phones. As phones are added, the number of possible connections rises almost as fast as the number of phones squared. [This contrast between the change in cost and value of a network as it grows is called 'Metcalfe's Law.] Any person with a phone can reach more people, so the network's value to them increases. Similarly, as the number of people online has grown, so has the value of being online to each Internet user. Moreover, as the Internet gains popularity, its technological specifications have become a default standard, encouraging new hardware and software innovations that use Internet technology as a platform." *Digital*

Economy 2000, June 2000, 4. See also Shapiro and Varian, *Information Rules*, 1999, 184; and Jean Tirole, *The Theory of Industrial Organization* (Cambridge, MA: MIT Press, 1992), 405: "A network externality arises when a good becomes more valuable to a user if the more users adopt the same good or compatible ones."

[82] Don Tapscott, *The Digital Economy* (NY: McGraw-Hill, 1996), 60.

[83] Frances Cairncross, *The Death of Distance: How the Communications Revolution Will Change Our Lives* (Boston: Harvard Business School Press, 1997), xi.

[84] Michael E. Porter, "Clusters and the New Economics of Competition," *Harvard Business Review*, November-December 1998, 77.

[85] See Richard Florida, *Competing in the Age of Talent: Environment, Amenities, and the New Economy*, A Report Prepared for the R.K. Mellon Foundation, Heinz Endowments, and Sustainable Pittsburgh, January 2000.

[86] Carly Fiornia, "Presentation at Winter NGA meeting, February 27, 2000; available at NGA web site: www.nga.org/2000Winter/Fiornia.asp.

[87] Ross C. DeVol with Perry Wong, John Catapano and Greg Robitshek, *America's High-Tech Economy: Growth, Development, and Risks for Metropolitan Areas* (Santa Monica, CA: Milken Institute, July 13, 1999, 9.

[88] See Alan A. Altshuler and Marc D. Zegans, "Innovation and Public Management: Notes from the State House and City Hall," In Alan A. Altshuler and Robert D. Behn, editors, *Innovation in American Government* (Washington: D.C.: Brookings, 1997).

[89] See Michael W. Cox and Richard Alm, *Myths of Rich & Poor: Why We're Better Off* (NY: Basic Books, 1999).

[90] See Erik Brynjolfsson and Lorin M. Hitt, "Beyond the Productivity Paradox: Computers are the Catalyst for Bigger Changes," *Communications of the ACM*, August 1998; as cited in *Digital Economy 2000*. 41.

[91] Philip Evans and Thomas W. Wurster, *Blown to Bits: How the New Economics of Information Transforms Strategy* (Boston: Harvard Business School Press, 2000), x-xi.

[92] See Thomas L. Friedman, "Next, It's Education," *New York Times*, November 17, 1999.

[93] David Osborne and Ted Gaebler, *Reinventing Government" How the Entrepreneurial Spirit is Transforming the Public Sector* (Reading, MA: Addison-Wesley, 1992).

[94] Michael Hammer and James Campy, *Reengineering the Corporation: A Manifesto for Business Revolution* (NY: HarperBusiness, 1993).

[95] Jerry Mechling, "Reengineering: Part of Your Game Plan?" *Governing*, February 1994).

[96] For a good primer on state web pages, see Thomas Unruh, "States on the Internet," National Governors' Association, February 26, 2000; available at www.nga.org/Pubs/IssueBriefs/2000/000226StatesInternet.asp.

[97] For more examples, see Steve Towns, "States Progress Toward Digital Nation," *Government Technology*, September 1998, 22-4. The full report was prepared by the Progress and Freedom Foundation in association with Government Technology.

[98] Steve Towns, "The Dawn of Electronic States," *Government Technology*, January 2000, 21.

[99] Tod Newcombe, "CIO: Does it Still Mean 'Career Is Over?'" *Government Technology*, July 1999, 12.

[100] "Competition for technology employees," Associated Press, November 28, 1999.

[101] Ciaran Ryan, "Blueprint for E-Government," *Government Technology: E Commerce*, August 1999, 26.

[102] Elizabeth Wasserman, "The County Clerk Moves to the Web," *The Industry Standard*, September 27, 1999, 44.

[103] Philip Evans and Thomas S. Wurster, *Blown to Bits: How the New Economics of Information Transforms Strategy* (Boston: Harvard Business School Press, 2000), 196.

[104] Michael Schrage, *Serious Play: How the World's Best Companies*

Simulate to Innovate (Boston: Harvard Business School Press, 2000), 101.
[105] John D. Donahue, *The Privatization Decision: Public Ends, Private Means* (NY: Basic Books, 1989), 3–7.
[106] See John Kost, *New Approaches to Public Management: The Case of Michigan* (Washington, D.C.: Center for Public Management, Brookings Institution, July 1996).
[107] David Osborne and Peter Plastrik, *Banishing Bureaucracy: The Five Strategies for Reinventing Government* (Reading, MA: Addison-Wesley, 1996), 143.
[108] Harry P. Hatry, *Performance Measurement: Getting Results* (Washington, D.C.: Urban Institute, 1999), 3.
[109] John E. Brandl, *Money and Good Intentions are Not Enough or Why a Liberal Democrat Thinks States Need Both Competition and Community* (Washington, D.C.: Brookings, 1998, 2–5.
[110] Virginia Postrel, *The Future and Its Enemies: The Growing Conflict Over Creativity, Enterprise, and Progress* (NY: Free Press, 1998), 45.
[111] David Osborne and Ted Gaebler, *Reinventing Government* (NY: Addison-Wesley, 1992).
[112] Thomas W. Bonnett, *Is the New Global Economy Leaving State-Local Tax Structures Behind?* (Washington, D.C.: National League of Cities, 1998).
[113] "No one controls the Internet," wrote Thomas W. Malone in the *Harvard Business Review*. "No one's in charge. No one's the leader. The Internet grew out of the combined efforts of all its users, with no central management. The Internet *had* to be self-managed." As quoted in Fred Andrews, "Merger Mania Got You Down? So, Start Thinking Small," *New York Times*, December 1, 1999, C14. Also see: ccs.mit.edu/21c.
[114] Walter Kiechel, "The New New Capital Thing," *Harvard Business Review*, July-August 2000, 150; also see Robert D. Putnam, *Bowling Alone: The Collapse and Revival of American Community* (NY: Simon & Schuster, 2000.
[115] As quoted in Alan K. Campbell, "Revisiting Metropolitanism

and Fiscal Disparities," *Journal of Policy Analysis and Management*, Vol.11, no.3, 370 (1992).

[116] As quoted in Roger Vaughan, Robert Pollard, and Barbara Dyer, *The Wealth of States: Policies for a Dynamic Economy* (Washington, D.C.: CSPA, 1985), 58. See also W.W. Rostow, *Theorists of Economic Growth from David Hume to the Present* (NY: Oxford University Press, 1990), 169:
Clearly, Marshall regarded increased outlays for education in England of his day as a form of investment subject to increasing returns. His analysis—and its predecessor analyses back to Hume and Adam Smith—makes it difficult to regard the emergence of investment in "human capital" in post-1945 development economics as a pioneering revelation."

[117] Peter F. Drucker, *People and Performance: The Best of Peter Drucker on Management* (NY: Harper & Row, 1977), 94.

[118] Special Section on Education, *Wall Street Journal*, February 9, 1990. See also *America's Choice: high skills or low wages!* Report of the Commission on the Skills of the American Workforce (Rochester, NY: National Center on Education and the Economy, June 1990).

[119] Anthony Patrick Carnevale, *America and the New Economy* (Alexandria, VA: American Society for Training and Development, U.S. Department of Labor, 1991), 1–2.

[120] As cited in Bruce Ackerman and Anne Alstott, *The Stakeholder Society* (New Haven, CT: Yale University Press, 1999), 238.

[121] Lynn A. Karoly et al, *Investing in Our Children* (Santa Monica, CA: Rand, 1998.

[122] Diane Ravitch, "Somebody's Children," Diane Ravitch and Joseph P. Viteritti, editors, *New Schools for a New Century: The Redesign of Urban Education* (New Haven, CT: Yale University Press, 1997), 255.

[123] Stan Davis and Jim Botkin, "The Coming of Knowledge-Based Business," *Harvard Business Review*, September-October 1994.

[124] Patrick Barta, "In Current Expansion, As Business Booms, So, Too, Do Layoffs," *Wall Street Journal*, March 12, 2000.

[125] Robert D. Atkinson, Randolph H. Court, and Joseph M. Ward, *The State New Economy Index* (Washington, D.C.: Progressive Policy Institute, July 1999), 22.

[126] Peter T. Kilborn, "Innovative Program in California Aids Those With Outdated Skills," *New York Times*, November 27, 1992, D7.

[127] Jackson Toby, "Getting Serious about School Discipline," *The Public Interest*, no. 133 (1998), 81.

[128] "IDAs are savings accounts that provide new incentives through matching funds and are not counted against low-income families when calculating social assistance eligibility. IDAs typically are managed by community agencies, and require financial advising as well as a cosigner when any funds are withdrawn. Funds can be only withdrawn for home purchase, education, investments in small businesses, or emergencies. Currently, the programs are small and experimental, but they are growing. Like all new programs many issues remain to be worked out, but at a minimum they help put wealth ownership back on the map as a way of helping poor individuals move up the wealth ladder. The recent welfare reform legislation has allowed states to use their federal block grant funds to support IDAs. In addition, private foundations, such as the Ford Foundation, are supporting programs such as "Downpayments on American Dreams," which provide IDAs as a way to develop savings for more people." C. Eugene Steuerle, Edward M. Gramlich, Hugh Heclo, and Demetra Smith Nightingale, *The Government We Deserve: responsive democracy and changing expectations* (Washington, D.C.: Urban Institute Press, 1998), 142–43. See also Michael Sherraden et al, *Saving Patterns in IDA Programs* (St.Louis: Center for Social Development, George Warren Brown School of Social Work, Washington University, January 2000).

[129] See Robert A. Caro, *The Power Broker: Robert Moses and the Fall of New York* (NY: Vintage, 1975); Kenneth T. Jackson, *Crabgrass Frontier: The Suburbanization of the United States* (NY: Oxford University Press, 1985); and Norquist (1998).

[130] See Thomas W. Bonnett and Robert L. Olson, "How Scenarios Enrich Public Policy Decisions," In Liam Fahey and Robert M. Randall, editors, *Learning From the Future: Competitive Foresight Scenarios* (NY: John Wiley & Sons, 1998).

[131] See Bruce Katz and Jennifer Bradley, "Divided We Sprawl," *The Atlantic Monthly*, December 1999.

[132] See Joel S. Hirschhorn, *Growing Pains: Quality of Life in the New Economy* (Washington, D.C.: National Governors' Association, 2000).

[133] Here is the conventional assessment: "Although the number of homes with computers and Internet connections have been rising rapidly, the majority of Americans do not have online connections at home. Those on the wrong side of the digital divide—disproportionately people with lower incomes, less education, and members of minority groups—are missing out on increasingly valuable opportunities for education, job search, and communication with their families and communities." *Digital Economy* 2000, vii. For an unconventional view, see Daniel Akst, "My Old Computer Can Bridge the Digital Divide," *Wall Street Journal*, August 9, 2000. According to Akst, "The real divide here isn't digital, it's educational."

[134] Note these examples present the traditional approaches by government to assist network industries: substantial subsidies to the railroads in the 19th century (in the form of hundreds of millions of acres of federal land given to them), regulatory policy in communications, and generous federal financing to build the Interstate Highway Defense System. Consider this observation as a stark contrast: "In the last decade policymiakers have privatized the Internet, employed auctions to reallocate the electromagnetic spectrum to higher value uses such as cellular telephony, and eliminated all prohibitions on entry in local telephony." Christopher Weare, Book Review, *Journal of Policy Analysis and Management* Vol.19, no.3 (Summer 2000), 496.

[135] On the topic of strategies, see Bob Rowe, "Strategies to Promote Advanced Telecommunications Capabilities," *Federal*

Communications Law Journal, March 2000, Vol. 52, no. 2; CC Docket No. 98–146, Federal Communications Commission, February 18, 2000; and Deborah Hurley and James H. Keller, editors, *The First 100 Feet: Options for Internet and Broadband Access* (Cambridge, MA: MIT Press, 1999). Some communities have established municipally owned local telephone companies to obtain advances services: for example, the Manning Municipal Communication and Television Systems Utility "now provides residents with cable television, high-speed Internet connections and, starting later this summer, improved telephone services, including voice mail, three-way calling, speed dialing and call forwarding, that have not been available. These telecommunications services, Ms. Phillips said, would have arrived only slowly, if at all, from GTE." Joel Kotkin, "Downloading Some Life Back Into Downtown," *New York Times*, June 18, 2000, BU 6.

[136] Charles Dervarics, "Fiber Optic Technology Modernizes Minnesota Roadways," *E Gov Journal*, November/December 1999, 8.

[137] Roger Vaughan, Robert Pollard, and Barbara Dyer, *The Wealth of States: Policies for a Dynamic Economy* (Washington, D.C.: Council of State Planning Agencies, 1985), 2.

[138] See Peter S. Fisher and Alan H. Peters, *Industrial Incentives: Competition Among American States and Cities* (W.E. Upjohn Institute, 1998).

[139] Galen Gruman, "A Governor's Tech Crusade," *Upside*, February 2000, 126.

[140] Michael Lewis, "The Search Engine," *New York Times Magazine*, October 10, 1999, 80.

[141] Richard R. Nelson and Paul M. Romer, "Science, economic growth, and public policy," *Challenge*, March 13, 1996., citing Zvi Griliches' work.

[142] Everett M. Rogers, *Diffusion of Innovations*, (NY: Free Press, 1995); see the Hybrid Corn Study and the Diffusion Paradigm, 53.

¹⁴³ See Louis G. Tornatzky, "Building State Economies By Promoting University-Industry Technology Transfer," Policy Brief, (Washington, D.C.: National Governors' Association, 2000); available at <www.nga.org/Center>.

¹⁴⁴ Dan Berglund and Marianne Clark, "Using Research and Development to Grow State Economies," Policy Brief, (Washington, D.C.: National Governors' Association, 2000); available at <www.nga.org/Center>.

¹⁴⁵ For a strong argument that commercially sponsored research is undermining the primary mission of higher education, see Eyal Press and Jennifer Washburn, "The Kept University," *The Atlantic Monthly*, March 2000; also see Richard Florida, "The Role of the University: Leveraging Talent, Not Technology," *Issues in Science and Technology*, Summer 1999: "If federal, state, and local policymakers really want to leverage universities to spawn economic growth, they must adopt a new view. They have to stop encouraging matches between university and industry for their own sake. Instead, they must focus on strengthening the university's ability to attract the smartest people from around the world—the true wellspring of the knowledge economy."

¹⁴⁶ Nelson and Romer, "Science, economic growth, and public policy."

¹⁴⁷ Robyn Meredith, "Tobacco Money Goes to Medical Research," *New York Times*, July 20, 1999, A10.

¹⁴⁸ See Nicholas Wade, "Genetic Code of Human Life is Cracked by Scientists," *New York Times*, June 27, 2000.

¹⁴⁹ Julia Flynn, "Gap Exists Between Entrepreneurship in Europe, North America, Study Shows," *Wall Street Journal*, July 2, 1999.

¹⁵⁰ Rev. Nathaniel Craigmiles, "Funeral Directors Close Lid on Competition," *Investor's Business Daily*, November 19, 1999.

¹⁵¹ See also Thom Rubel and Scott Palladino, "Nurturing Entrepreneurial Growth in State Economies," Policy Brief, (Washington, D.C.: National Governors' Association, 2000); available at <www.nga.org/Center>.

[152] Don Clark, "Spurred by Tech Frenzy, Venture Firms Set Records in Investments Last Year," *Wall Street Journal*, February 7, 2000.
[153] See Robert G. Heard and John Sibert, "Growing New Businesses with Seed and Venture Capital: State Experiences and Options, Policy Brief, (Washington, D.C.: National Governors' Association, 2000); available at <www.nga.org/Center>.
[154] Michael E. Porter, *On Competition* (Boston: Harvard Business Review, 1999), 322–3.
[155] See Joseph Cortright and Heike Mayer, "The Ecology of the Silicon Forest," unpublished paper, Regional Connections Project, Institute for Portland Metropolitan Studies, Portland State University.
[156] In addition to Porter's work, see John M. Redman, *Understanding State Economies Through Industry Studies* (Washington, D.C.: Council of Governors' Policy Advisors, 1994); available through NGA publications..
[157] Annalee Saxenian, *Regional Advantage: Culture and Competition in Silicon Valley and Route 128* (Cambridge, MA: Harvard University Press, 1998), 9.
[158] Michael E. Porter, "Clusters and the New Economics of Competition," *Harvard Business Review*, November-December 1998, 78.
[159] See John M. Redman, *Understanding State Economies Through Industry Studies* (Washington, D.C.: Council of Governors' Policy Advisors, 1994); available through NGA publications.
[160] As quoted in Neil Scott Kleiman, "The Sector Solution," (NY: Center for an Urban Future, January 2000).
[161] Saxenian, *Regional Advantage*.
[162] Michael Best, *The New Competition: Institutions of Industrial Restructuring* (Cambridge, MA: Harvard University Press, 1990), 13.
[163] Thomas W. Bonnett, *Is the New Global Economy Leaving State-Local Tax Structures Behind?* (Washington, D.C.: National League of Cities, 1998).
[164] See "Total State and Local Tax Rate on Sales of Telecommunica-

tion Services: Committee on State Taxation 50-State Study and Report on Telecommunications Taxation," (Washington, D.C.: Committee on State Taxation, September 7, 1999. Also see Thomas W. Bonnett, *TELEWARS in the States: Telecommunications Issues in a New Era of Competition* (Washington, D.C.: Council of Governors' Policy Advisors, 1996), 116:

> For most of this century, telephone companies were regulated monopolies. As such, they and other public utilities were convenient sources of revenue for state and local governments. Indeed, regulators generally allowed taxes on public utilities to be passed through to the ratepayers. State and local taxes had little incidence on corporate profits, because regulators were using rate of return (not unlike a cost-plus approach) to set telephone and utility rates. This was a sweet deal for state and local administrators. Few companies protested very long or very hard, because most of the tax burden was simply passed along.

[165] See Scott Palladino and Stacy Mazer, "Telecommunications Tax Policies: Implications for the Digital Age," National Governors' Association, February 2000.

[166] See Thomas W. Bonnett, "Taxing (and Not Taxing) Electronic Commerce, *State Tax Notes*, November 1, 1999; and "Retail E-Commerce Threatens to Erode Public Sector Revenues," *Nation's Cities Weekly*, November 29, 1999.

[167] The Monthly Retail Trade Survey, the source of this estimate, "includes only retail firms. It excludes non-retail operations such as travel agencies, financial services, manufacturers, and wholesalers." See Monthly Retail Trade Survey; Frequently Asked Questions (FAQ). Available at <www.census.gov/mrts/www/faq.html>. See also U.S. Department of Commerce News, "Retail E-Commerce Sales Are $5.3 Billion in First Quarter 2000, Census Bureau Reports, May 31, 2000. This is embarrassing. It is either tragically stupid or comically absurd. These estimates do not include any electronic commerce between firms identified as manufacturers and the consumer. Dell Computer and IBM are manufacturing firms, according to their

SIC codes. Hence, their e-retail sales directly to consumers are not included in these estimates.

[168] Gerald R. Seib and Jim VandeHei, "A Lobbying Machine Springs Up to Revive Issue of Internet Taxes," *Wall Street Journal*, June 29, 2000, A10.

[169] Donald Bruce and William F. Fox, "E-Commerce in the Context of Declining State Sales Tax Bases," unpublished paper, April 2000, University of Tennessee, Knoxville, TN; see also "Sales Taxes: Electronic Commerce Growth Presents Challenges; Revenue Losses are Uncertain," United States General Accounting Office, June 2000, GAO/GGD/OCE-00-165.

[170] Corporate income taxes provided 8.7 percent of all state revenues in 1948, 7.6 percent in 1979; and 7 percent in 1997. For the latter figure, see John Donahue, *disunited States* (NY: Basic Books, 1997), 238.

[171] John Due argued the perception of high or burdensome business taxes is more harmful to a positive business climate than the actual burden imposed by them: "The endless propaganda on the subject and strategy-inspired announcements of business firms when tax changes are being considered lead many legislators to exaggerate the influence of the taxes beyond any effect which they may have. The result is a potential danger of state cut-throat competition. . . . In terror of "driving business out," legislatures become unwilling to adjust taxes to levels necessary to meet the desires of the community for services, and to bring their tax structures in line with popularly accepted ideas of equity in taxation." John F. Due, "Studies of State-Local Tax Influences on Location of Industry," *National Tax Journal*, Vol. XIV, no. 2, 1961, 171.

[172] Bonnett, *Is the New Global Economy Leaving State-Local Tax Structures Behind?*

[173] Aaron Wildavsky, *Searching for Safety* (New Brunswick, NJ: Transaction Publishers, 1988), 91.

[174] Paul Romer, "Innovation: The New Pump of Growth," *Blue-*

print: Ideas for a New Century (Washington, D.C.: Democratic Leadership Council, Winter 1998).

[175] Keynote Address by Scott McNealy, in O'Reilly & Associates, eds. *The Harvard Conference on the Internet and Society* (Cambridge, MA: Harvard University Press, 1996), 50.

[176] See *State Strategies for the New Economy*, Issue Brief, (Washington, D.C.: National Governors' Association, 2000), 41.

APPENDIX A

Will Retail E-commerce Erode Public Sector Revenues?[1]

At the September 1999 meeting of the Advisory Commission on Electronic Commerce, its chairman, Virginia Governor James Gilmore, asked an excellent question of a panel of state and local elected officials. His question was "If the sales tax has been able to withstand the growth of mail order sales, why do you think it will not survive the emergence of electronic commerce?"

A full answer requires a historical perspective. In 1967, when the Supreme Court ruled on the *Bellas Hess* case, the median (half above, half below) state sales tax rate was 3 percent. The court ruled that Illinois could not require a remote vendor to collect the state sales/use tax because the firm lacked a physical presence, called nexus, in that state.[2] State officials were concerned with the 1967

---

[1] This is adapted from an opinion article printed in *Nation's Cities Weekly*, National League of Cities, November 29, 1999. Used by permission.

[2] The Court upheld the *Bellas Hess* ruling in the 1992 *Quill* case, but on narrower grounds. The *Quill* decision made it clear that Congress, with its authority to regulate interstate commerce, can establish the terms governing the burden to collect the state sales/use tax. From the last paragraph of *Quill*: "Accordingly, Congress is now free to decide, whether, when and to what extent the States may burden interstate mail-order concerns with a duty to collect use taxes."

court ruling because they felt it was unfair to the Mom and Pop retailers on Main Street that had to collect the state sales/use tax.

No one at that time expected mail-order shopping to grow so remarkably. The U.S. Advisory Commission on Intergovernmental Relations estimated a public-sector revenue loss of $3.3 billion in 1994 from untaxed mail-order sales. According to the Direct Marketing Association, catalog sales have increased by 8.6 percent annually between 1994 and 1999.

The median state sales tax is now 5 percent. Why is it so much higher than thirty years ago? States need a higher rate today to raise sufficient revenues because the tax base is not growing as fast as the national economy. People are spending proportionately less money on goods and more on services, which are seldom taxed. Plus, today more spending flows to remote vendors, who do not have the responsibility to collect the sales/use tax.

The other big difference from thirty years ago is how many local jurisdictions rely on the sales tax as a revenue source. In 1967, only a few big cities had the authority to collect a local sales tax. Today, approximately 6600 local governments tax sales, usually piggybacked on the state tax. Hence, the sales tax generates about 16 percent of local governments' tax-revenues, in addition to about one-third of the state tax revenues.

Sharing this revenue source with local governments has boosted the total average tax rates. The combined average state/local sales tax rate was 6.74 in 1981; it crept up to 8.25 percent in 1998. (Five states do not use sales taxes so the national average is 6.1 percent.) Indeed, the combined state and local rates in a few jurisdictions have reached 11 percent. High sales tax rates encourage the most price-sensitive shoppers to avoid the tax burden by crossing borders or buying from remote vendors. Mail-order sales have grown rapidly because of this non-tax, price advantage and because it has become a very convenient and reliable way for adults in busy households to shop.

> **"History does not repeat itself, it rhymes,"** as Mark Twain may have written.
>
> John Quelch, the Dean of the London Business School, made a comparison of mail-order sales to online shopping in the *HARVARD BUSINESS REVIEW* (July-August 1999, 162).
>
> "Naysayers' reaction to the Net are similar to those we heard 15 or 20 years ago from the United States when direct mail catalogs started to become more prominent. One common preconception about direct mail was that it would work only with certain products. Another was that it was unreliable, that buying through the mail was too risky for consumers. Still another assumption was that if a retailer engaged in direct mail, catalog sales would cannibalize store sales. Do those reactions sound familiar? Well, all three proved to be myths, and— as they relate to e-commerce— all three will again, given time."
>
> Dean Quelch concludes, "We just don't know what can and will be sold over the Net." Shifting from economics to sociology, what is the most valuable commodity in any two-income family? If it is not money, it is time. Retail e-commerce is clearly following the path blazed by mail-order sales to become a convenient and reliable way to shop.
>
> Time is valuable, so why wouldn't the harried 100 million Americans with Internet access use this medium for retail shopping as well? Well, of course they will. Online shoppers spent an estimated $9 billion during the 1999 holiday season. Amazon.com reports having had 14 million visitors to its web site in one month (January 2000).

So, the short answer to Governor Gilmore's excellent question is this: the sales tax survived its shrining tax base and the growth of mail-order sales by raising its rates. But the higher rates have pushed price-sensitive consumers into tax avoidance—more mail-order and more online shopping.

A higher tax on a shrinking tax base is bad medicine for any tax. This is why many public finance experts fear that electronic commerce will erode the future revenue stream from the sales tax.

The public in the 21st century will continue to demand quality services. Those services will require a balanced array of taxes, including a state/local sales tax applied equally to all forms of shopping. That means that remote vendors should be given an expanded duty to collect the sales/use tax, putting them on equal footing with the Mom and Pop retailers on Main Street and in the malls.

The failure to achieve this tax equity principle could undermine the future viability of the sales tax, jeopardizing the autonomy of state and local governments. Expanding the duty to collect the state sales tax to remote vendors and simplifying this tax to achieve uniformity among the states is the best strategy to end the current policy stalemate, and to preserve federalism in the 21st century. (See also <www.nga.org/releases.pr-16November1999Proposal>.)

APPENDIX B

PANDERING.COM, or

Battle Not Lost, War Not Won[3]

The Advisory Commission on Electronic Commission, appointed by Congress to make recommendations on tax policy, concluded its formal meetings and made its final report to Congress in the spring of 2000. Most news reports focused on the drama of the last meeting in Dallas, but the richer, more engaging story is how this obscure issue—due to presidential neglect—grew into a bare-knuckle brawl.

The March meeting in Dallas ended with bitterness and rancor. Some of the public sector members—Utah Governor Leavitt and Dallas Mayor Kirk—accused the business caucus of being more concerned with protecting special advantages for their own firms than supporting the principle of tax equity.[4] Be that as it may, the business caucus does not bear the major burden for the failure of the ACEC to recommend to Congress that it must establish a level playing field for electronic commerce.

---

[3] Adapted from the version posted at <www.gma.com/features/ecommerce/pandering.shtml>.

[4] "'Six pigs at the trough,' is how one frustrated state representative characterized the business members of the Gilmore Commission," wrote David Ignatius, "E-execs in loophole heaven," *Washington Post*, March 29, 2000.

Perhaps the last-minute shift of the business caucus to the anti-tax side reflected the "nature of business," but I demur. Each of the 19 people on this Commission was a volunteer, and serving on it was a thankless and frustrating task. To some social critics, the inability of the business caucus to act as stewards of the public interest provides a harsh commentary on our pallid civic culture.[5] **But, should we expect these corporate executives to be enlightened angels[6] when our national politicians are obsessed with pandering to special interests?** Hardly.

Was ACEC a "Stacked Deck?"

Here are the reasons why many public-sector observers think this commission was rigged from the start:

- Questionable appointments to the ACEC, including the failure to comply with the law that prompted a legal challenge by the

---

[5] When Judis quotes Woodson Wilson in 1912 saying, "[t]he business of government is to organize the common interest against the special interests," it resonates with integrity, yet sounds quaint. See John B. Judis, *The Paradox of American Democracy* (NY: Pantheon, 2000).

[6] "But what is government itself but the greatest of all reflections on human nature? If men were angels, no government would be necessary. If angels were to govern men, neither external nor internal controls on government would be necessary. In framing a government which is to be administered by men over men, the great difficulty lies in this: You must first enable the government to controul the governed; and in the next place, oblige it to controul itself." *The Federalist* No. 51, at 322 (James Madison) (1788) (Jacob E. Cooke, ed., Wesleyan University Press, 1961).

National Association of Counties and the Mayors group, and the appointment of a member who serves as a partisan advisor to the Congressional leadership and is a paid lobbyist for Microsoft. (They were the last act of Speaker Gingrich; thanks Newt.)

- No initial public funding for the Commission's work, which prevented it from developing its own research agenda.

- The requirement that the "findings and recommendations" receive a two-thirds vote of the Commission, a feature insisted upon by the Republican leaders in Congress.

- The executive director, chosen by the Chair, Governor James Gilmore of Virginia, accepted rent-free space from the Electronic Industries Alliance prior to its first meeting. At that time, her husband was Vice President of this trade association, whose members are very interested in this issue. Her annual salary was greater than that of the director of the CIA.

- Governor Gilmore's supervision of the commission staff was lacking. One afternoon session was dominated by anti-tax ideologues, and one presenter was allowed to discuss a telecommunications issue (open access-forced access of cable TV systems) that had absolutely no bearing on the Commission's work.[7]

- The curious dinner in New York City, financed by selective corporate sponsors without the members' prior knowledge or consent. Private sector sponsors paid $10,000 per table or $5,000 for four seats to have special access to the commissioners, many of whom had no idea the event was being used

---

[7] See John Judis, "Republicans hijack the e-commerce debate," *The New Republic*, October 11, 1999.

to raise funds or how they would be spent. The executive director denied the dinner was a fund-raiser, conceded that dinner contributions totaled $40,000 to $50,000, and maintained that any leftover funds would be given back to various sponsors on a pro-rated basis.[8]

You either laugh or cry at this explanation. O.K., so dinner in Manhattan is expensive. But if this event was not a fundraiser, why the steep ticket price? And, who was invited to have dinner with the commissioners?

Michael Mazerov of the Center for Budget and Policy Priorities, who told the Commission that web shoppers have incomes twice the national average, was not invited. The skeptics justifiably wonder, "Would the surplus have been returned to the private sponsors if this story had not first appeared in *State Tax Notes* soon after this dinner?"

None of these curiosities is a smoking gun. But, taken together, they undermine the credibility of the ACEC's effort. The commission failed by design, and by its own incompetence. The ACEC was created because the President and Congress wanted to impose a tax moratorium to pander to Silicon Valley and its running buddies, AOL and Microsoft. They accepted the idea of a commission as a concession to public sector leaders, and then stacked the deck with dubious appointments and rigged the process.

The Emperor's New Clothes

Few readers will remember President Clinton's speech to Silicon Valley executives in February 1998 in which he supported the

---

[8] Doug Sheppard, "Industry Groups Sponsor Dinner for Federal E-Commerce Panel," *State Tax Notes*, September 23, 1999.

moratorium on taxing Internet transactions and claimed that he did not want the Internet to become "a tax haven."[9] He must have been infected with "goof-gas," that sinister invention of Boris and Natasha that made everyone talk nonsense, leaving Bullwinkle "the smart one on the show" he shared with Rocky J. Squirrel.

That anyone, much less the President, could make both statements simultaneously illustrates how few people really understood this issue two years ago. It also reveals how uncritical the media has been on technology issues.

Why did not others point out the emperor wore no clothes? Most national politicians were too busy touring the Valley to shake down the new wealth from those creating *The New, New Thing*, as Michael Lewis brilliantly portrays in his latest book.[10] And where was the precious Fourth Estate? Covering a very different kind of story, indeed.

The only consistent voices in 1998 saying that a tax moratorium on Internet access fees and transactions would create an electronic *tax haven* were a handful of public sector leaders who understood that their future budgets were vulnerable because they depend upon sales tax revenues. Sales taxes generate one-third of state revenues and sixteen percent of local government revenues, or roughly one-quarter of all state-local tax revenues.[11]

---

[9] Remarks of the President to Technology '98 Conference, San Francisco, February 28, 1998.

[10] Michael Lewis, *The New New Thing: A Silicon Valley Story* (NY: Norton, 2000).

[11] Harley T. Duncan, Executive Director of the Federation of Tax Administrators, presentation to the Advisory Commission on Electronic Commerce, September 15, 2000.

And those intrepid leaders were often denounced as being greedy, anti-progress, and "evil" by the industry-financed flacks.

The Tide is Turning, Slowly...

When the governors had their winter 2000 meeting in Washington, D.C., President Clinton told them he was opposed to extending the tax moratorium. He offered to negotiate with the governors and the industry leaders to resolve this conflict. All that time with Dick Morris must have affected his concept of presidential leadership. After selling state and local governments short in 1998, did he think he could redeem himself by offering to negotiate? No one pursued his offer.

Corporate executives in the New Economy are experiencing similar conflicts. Steven Case of AOL told the *New York Times* that Internet commerce should be taxed no differently than any other sales at the same time AOL's chief strategist was in Dallas pushing the ACEC to recommend extending the tax moratorium until 2006.

Bill Gates has been generous in giving billions to charity. Both Gates and Case know the value of their brand is the most valuable asset of their companies. In this knowledge economy, many services have become relationships between consumers and providers. Having a positive brand image ("friendly, pro-community, and generous") is worth cultivating through advertising and supporting good works. The risk of backlash should be too great for their companies to be perceived by the public as playing hard-ball politics in their efforts to twist public policies into self-serving pretzels.

Some observers think AOL and Microsoft are learning how to find surrogates to do the heavy lifting in public policy trenches to preserve their reputations.[12] Others argue they still have not learned this important lesson. [13]

As Issue Matures, the Public Learns

Two years ago, my public finance monograph observed, "The sponsors of the Internet Tax Freedom Act have performed, inadvertently, a valuable public service. Attention focused on this legislation has helped many state and local policymakers understand the potential threat of the loss of sales tax revenues from electronic commerce."[14]

And that has been the major benefit of the Advisory Commission on Electronic Commerce. Its hearings, its controversies, its bumbling, and even its inability to recommend to Congress

---

[12] Microsoft contributes to a variety of organizations, some of which generate reports intended to influence public opinion in support of the policy preferences of Microsoft. This was not a coincidence, as we learned when Oracle admitted hiring the Investigative Group International, a private detective agency, "to investigate numerous Microsoft front organizations." See John Markoff and Matt Richtel, *New York Times*, June 28, 2000. Both AOL and Microsoft have employed IGI in the past to gather competitive intelligence. See also Ted Bridis, Glenn Simpson, and Mylene Mangalindan, "How Piles of Trash Became Latest Focus in Gates-Ellison Feud," *Wall Street Journal*, June 29, 2000.

[13] For example, it would be hard to miss the on-going conflict between Microsoft's aggressive business strategy ("Embrace, Extend, Extinguish") and federal antitrust policy.

[14] Thomas W. Bonnett, *Is the New Global Economy Leaving State-Local Tax Structures Behind?* (Washington, D.C.: National League of Cities, 1998).

that all sales be treated equally—all the hustle and bustle of its sixteen months of existence helped educate the public that the existing tax structure is woefully inept, and requires a major overhaul.

Just a few years ago, most public officials did not understand the nexus rule established by the Supreme Court, electronic commerce, or the potential loss of public sector revenues. And, the general public thought the Internet was a youth phenomenon like pierced earrings, nose rings, and pink hair. Today, Governors, Mayors, and County Executives are competing against each other to build the best web page.

More importantly, the public is beginning to understand that web shopping has special tax treatment, and it does not approve. A survey, commissioned by the U.S. Conference of Mayors and the National Association of Counties, found that 72 percent of Americans say it's unfair that online retailers do not collect sales taxes.

A poll by USAToday/CNN/Gallup earlier this year found that 65 percent thought "people should be required to pay the same sales tax for purchases made over the Internet as they would if they had bought the item in person at a local store." Just 28 percent disagreed.

A Scripps Howard poll found that "most Texans believe items bought over the Internet should be taxed as the same rate as purchases from brick-and-mortar stores." The poll found 49 percent use the Internet and 56 percent have home computers. Fifty-four percent of those surveyed said they favored equal tax rates, while 32 opposed them, and 14 percent declined to answer this question. [15]

---

[15] Jennifer Files, "Poll shows most Texans favor online sales tax," *The Dallas Morning News*, March 13, 2000.

Fifty-one percent of state revenues in Texas come from the sales tax, according to *Governing* magazine. Florida, the other state in the Bush leagues, gets 57 percent of its state tax revenue from the sales tax.[16]

News Flash to Congress—those who do not use the Internet are even more likely to think that web shopping should be taxed exactly the same as shopping in retail stores. As my 11-year son might say, "Duh!"

Just two years ago, the lobbyists for the America Online and its allies persuaded Congress that Internet access fees of this "infant industry" should be exempt from state and local taxes. In January 2000 AOL proposed a $165 billion merger with Time Warner, a global media powerhouse. "Some infant industry," one might respond sarcastically. From copping blatant tax privileges from Congress to gaining control of some of the most valuable media assets throughout the world—that was one great 14-month sprint for AOL and its leader, Steven Case.

Recent miracles notwithstanding, how can AOL—on its merits—convince Congress to extend the current tax moratorium on Internet access fees when 14 states impose the sales tax on computer information services and 11 states impose the tax on computer and data processing services?

Congress Hides on the Issue

Most members of Congress do not know the difference between a *"bit"* and a *"byte"* but they will learn soon enough that pandering to AOL, Silicon Valley and the *dot.coms* comes with heavy political baggage. Retailers and the local chambers of com-

---

[16] Christopher Swope, "E-conomics Problem," *Governing*, March 2000.

merce will be asking why they have to collect sales taxes for state and local governments while the high-flying *dot.coms* do not. As Utah Governor Michael Leavitt predicts, business executives and business owners will "besiege Capital Hill with one phrase on their lips—leveling playing field."[17]

Many in Congress will hide behind the black robes of the Supreme Court when confronted by their angry constituents: "Well, the court ruled that the states could not force the remote sellers to collect the sales/use tax because they lack a physical presence, called nexus, in that state."

This is the perfect answer to the wrong question. In its 1992 *Quill* decision, the Court said that Congress, with its authority to regulate interstate commerce, could establish the terms governing the burden to collect the sales/use tax. **Congress does not want to cast the tough vote to modify the** *Quill* **decision to achieve tax equity.** Furthermore, extending the tax moratorium sustains the flow of industry money into electoral campaigns.

A few in Congress will argue that the *dot.coms* should not have to pay any new taxes because the Internet is the best thing in America since "sliced bread." They may be right about the latter, but clearly are wrong about the former. Consumers pay the sales/use tax. The only public policy issue is whether remote sellers should have a responsibility to collect the sales tax (as do the Mom & Pop store owners on Main Street), and remit the revenues to the appropriate state/local jurisdiction. And modern technology should make that a snap.

---

[17] As Governor Leavitt predicted, the "bricks-and-mortar" retailers are beginning to make their voices heard on this tax equity issue. See Gerald F. Seib and Jim VandeHei, "A Lobbying Machine Springs Up to Revive Issue of Internet Taxes," *Wall Street Journal*, June 29, 2000.

Others in Congress will remind their constituents of their pledge against new taxes, and claim that applying taxes to web shopping is a new tax. Wrong again.

Every state with a sales tax also has an equivalent use tax. Consumers who purchase something outside their home state are responsible for taxing a use tax on it. If Jane buys a car out-of-state, she has to pay a use tax before she can register the car.

Most people do not report the use tax on their out-of-state purchases or those via telephone, catalogue, or Internet. North Carolina and Michigan added a special line on their state income tax forms in 1999 to remind everyone of his or her responsibility to pay this use tax.

Coming Attractions

The immediate future will mirror the recent past. Congress will avoid making a tough vote to establish tax equity among various sellers; as an institution, it benefits too much from the flow of industry money into campaigns.

In the spring of 2000, Speaker-hopeful Richard Gephardt announced his party's pandering package to the information technology industry, which included extending the tax moratorium until 2003. Hence, the Republican leadership, who want it extended until 2006, win the pandering contest.[18] So one might expect the tax moratorium to be extended.[19]

---

[18] Jim VanderHei, "Gephardt, Seeking to Boost Democrat's Image, Plans to Propose Tax Breaks for Internet Firms," March 28, 2000; and "GOP Seeks to Best Democrats on Web-Tax Delay," April 7, 2000, *Wall Street Journal*.

[19] "Without holding a single hearing, the House overwhelmingly approved a five-year extension of the e-commerce tax morato-

Long before 2003, the governors and mayors, concerned with the erosion of their revenue streams, will be joined on Capitol Hill by mobs of angry retailers. The tide will shift dramatically when corporate executives, sensitive to this inevitable public backlash, throw off the anti-tax armor to embrace a moderate "win-win" deal.

States reform their tax systems by establishing uniform definitions, rules, and simplifications while remote sellers assume the burden to collect the sales/use tax. The moderate proposal to establish a level-playing field among all sellers was what the business caucus backed away from at the last moment prior to the Dallas meeting.

Bigger Issues on Horizon

As this issue matures, policy makers should consider broader questions about how to achieve tax reform in the digital age.

What should be taxed in the future as production and consumption become disconnected from the tyranny of geography?

How do we create a fair, neutral tax system? One that does not discriminate for or against new technologies that improve productivity, enhance opportunity, and create wealth.

Can we preserve state and local autonomy when the networked economy pushes society toward uniform standards and common protocols?

---

rium, but Senate Republicans want to slow it down and scale it back. With politicians eager to please the booming Internet industry during an election year, the House rushed through legislation to extend the current moratorium until 2006." Jim VandeHei, "House Approves Tax Moratorium for Net Commerce," *Wall Street Journal*, May 11, 2000, B-12.

These are not questions that Regis Philbin is likely to ask on his popular TV show. Nor should we expect answers to spring forth in the 2000 presidential campaign. But we must ask our elected officials to take these tax questions seriously. Perhaps the best one might hope for, in the months and years ahead, is that civic leaders will engage in a broader discussion about these policy challenges—and not be distracted by the pandering of most of our national politicians and the self-interested policy agendas of the new emerging industry leaders of this digital age.

SELECTED BIBLIOGRAPHY

Adams, Scott. *The Dilbert Future: Thriving on Stupidity in the 21st Century* (NY: HarperBusiness, 1997).

Altschuler, Alan and Robert B. Behn, editors. *Innovation in American Government: Challenges, Opportunities, and Dilemmas* (Washington, D.C.: Brookings, 1997).

Barnes, William R. and Larry C. Ledebur. *The New Regional Economies* (Thousand Oaks, CA: Sage, 1998).

Barker, Lynton, David Carr, Joseph Kehoe and Ian Littman. *Transforming Government Services—A Global Perspective* (Mansfield, OH: PricewaterhouseCoopers, LLP, 1998).

Barry, Dave. *In Cyberspace* (NY: Crown Publishers, 1996).

Barry, John A. *Technobabble* (Cambridge, MA: MIT Press, 1993).

Bartik, Timothy J. *Who Benefits From State and Local Economic Development Policies?* (Kalamazoo, MI: W. E. Upjohn Institute for Employment Research, 1991).

Barzelay, Michael with Babak J. Armajani. *Breaking Through Bureaucracy: A New Vision for Managing in Government* (Berkeley, CA: University of California Press, 1992).

Beniger, James R. *The Control Revolution: Technological and Economic Origins of the Information Society* (Cambridge, MA: Harvard University Press, 1986).

Berners-Lee, Tim with Mark Fischetti. *Weaving the Web* (NY: HarperSanFrancisco, 1999).

Bernstein, Peter L. *Against the Gods: The Remarkable Story of Risk* (NY: Wiley, 1998).

Bhide, Amar V. *The Origin and Evolution of New Businesses* (NY: Oxford University Press, 2000).

Bonnett, Thomas W. *Governance in the Digital Age* and *Is the New Global Economy Leaving State-Local Tax Structures Behind?* (Washington, D.C.: National League of Cities, 1999 and 1998, respectively).

Bonnett, Thomas W. *TELEWARS in the States: Telecommunications Issues in a New Era of Competition* (Washington, D.C.: Council of Governors' Policy Advisors, 1996).

Brandl, John E. *Money and Good Intentions are Not Enough: Or, Why a Liberal Democrat Thinks States Need Both Competition and Community* (Washington, D.C.: Brookings, 1998).

Brown, John Seely and Paul Duguid. *The Social Life of Information* (Boston, MA: Harvard Business School Press, 2000).

Brunori, David, editor. *The Future of State Taxation* (Washington, D.C.: Urban Institute Press, 1998).

Burtless, Gary, Robert Z. Lawrence, Robert E. Litan, and Robert J. Shapiro. *Globaphobia: Confronting Fears about Open Trade* (Washington, D.C.: Brookings Institution, 1998).

Chancellor, Edward. *Devil Take the Hindmost: A History of Financial Speculation* (NY: Farrar, Strauss, Giroux, 1999).

Chandler, Alfred D., Jr. *Scale and Scope: The Dynamics of Industrial Capitalism* (Cambridge, MA: Harvard University Press, 1990).

Chernow, Ron. *Titan: The Life of John D. Rockefeller, Sr.* (NY: Random House, 1998).

Christensen, Clayton M. *The Innovator's Dilemma: When New Technologies Cause Great Firms to Fail* (Boston: Harvard Business School Press, 1997).

Cox, W. Michael and Richard Alm. *Myths of Rich & Poor: Why We're Better Off* (NY: Basic Books, 1999).

Dertouzos, Michael L. *What Will Be: How the New World of Information Will Change Our Lives* (NY: HarperEdge, 1997).

DeVol, Ross with Perry Wong, John Catapano and Greg Robitshek. *America's High-Tech Economy—Growth, Development, and Risks for Metropolitan Areas* (Santa Monica, CA: Milken Institute, July 13, 1999).

Downes, Larry and Chunka Mui. *Killer App: digital strategies for market dominance* (Boston: Harvard Business School Press, 1998).

Drucker, Peter F. *Innovation and Entrepreneurship* (Harper & Row, 1985).

Drucker, Peter F. *Post-Capitalist Society* (NY: Harper Business, 1993).

Eisinger, Peter K. *The Rise of the Entrepreneurial State: State and Local Economic Development Policy in the United States* (Madison, WI: University of Wisconsin Press, 1988).

Evans, Philip and Thomas S. Wurster. *Blown to Bits: How the New Economics of Information Transforms Strategy* (Boston: Harvard Business School Press, 2000).

Farrell, Winslow. *How Hits Happen* (NY: HarperBusiness, 1998).

Fingleton, Eamonn. *In Praise of Hard Industries: Why Manufacturing, not the Information Economy, is the Key to Future Prosperity* (NY: Houghton Mifflin, 1999).

Fisher, Peter S. and Alan H. Peters. *Industrial Incentives: Competition Among American States and Cities* (Kalamazoo, MI: W. E. Upjohn Institute for Employment Research, 1998).

Florida, Richard. *Competing in the Age of Talent—Environment, Amenities, and the New Economy*, A report prepared for the R. K. Mellon Foundation, Heinz Endowments, and Sustainable Pittsburgh. Carnegie Mellon University, Pittsburgh, PA.

Florida, Richard and Martin Kenney. *The Breakthrough Illusion* (NY: Basic Books, 1990).

Frank, Robert W. and Philip J. Cook. *The Winner-Take-All Society* (NY: Penguin, 1995).

Freeman, Richard B. and Peter Gottschalk, editors. *Generating Jobs: How to Increase Demand for Less-Skilled Workers* (NY: Russell Sage Foundation, 1998).

Friedman, Thomas L. *The Lexus and the Olive Tree: Understanding Globalization* (NY: Farrar, Straus, Giroux, 1999).

Fukuyama, Francis. *Trust: The Social Virtues & the Creation of Prosperity* (NY: Free Press, 1995).

Gates, Bill with Nathan Myhrvold and Peter Rinearson. *The Road Ahead* (NY: Penguin, 1996).

Gilder, George. *Microcosm* (NY: Simon & Schuster, 1989).
Gleick, James. *Faster: The Acceleration of Just About Everything* (NY: Pantheon, 1999).
Graham, Otis L. Jr. *Losing Time: The Industrial Policy Debate* (Cambridge, MA: Harvard University Press, 1992).
Greider, William. *One World, Ready or Not: The Manic Logic of Global Capitalism* (NY: Touchstone, 1997).
Hager, Barry M. *Limiting Risks and Sharing Losses in the Globalized Capital Market* (Washington, D.C.: Woodrow Wilson Center Press, 1998).
Hamel, Gary and C.K. Prahalad. *Competing For the Future* (Boston: Harvard Business School Press, 1994).
Hammer, Michael and James Champy. *Reengineering the Corporation: A Manifesto for Business Revolution* (NY: HarperBusiness, 1993).
Hampden-Turner, Charles and Alfons Trompenaars. *The Seven Cultures of Capitalism: Value Systems for Creating Wealth in the United States, Japan, Germany, France, Britain, Sweden, and the Netherlands* (NY: Currency/Doubleday, 1993).
Handy, Charles. *The Age of Unreason* (Boston: Harvard Business School Press, 1990).
Harrison, Bennett. *Lean & Mean: Why Large Corporations Will Continue to Dominate the Global Economy* (NY: Guilford Press, 1997).
Hiltzik, Michael. *Dealers of Lightning: XEROX PARC and the Dawn of the Computer Age* (NY: HarperBusiness, 1999).
Hirschhorn, Joel S. *Growing Pains: Quality of Life in the New Economy* (Washington, D.C.: National Governors' Association, 2000).
Hunt, Reed E. *You Say You Want a Revolution: A Story of Information Age Politics* (New Haven, CT: Yale University Press, 2000).
Hurley, Deborah and James H. Keller, editors. *The First 100 Feet: Options for Internet and Broadband Access* (Cambridge, MA: MIT Press, 1999).
Kamerman, Sheila B. and Alfred J. Kahn, *Privatization and the Welfare State* (Princeton, NJ: Princeton University Press, 1989).
Karoly, Lynn A., Peter W. Greenwood, Susan S. Everingham, Jill Hoube, M. Rebecca Kilburn, C. Peter Rydell, Matthew

Sanders, and James Chiesa. *Investing in Our Children: What We Know and Don't Know about the Costs and Benefits of Early Childhood Interventions* (Santa Monica, CA: Rand, 1998).

Kelly, Kevin. *New Rules for the New Economy* (NY: Penguin Books, 1998).

Kettl, Donald F. *Sharing Power: Public Governance and Private Markets* (Washington, D.C.: Brookings, 1993).

Kiel, L. Douglas. *Managing Chaos and Complexity in Government: A New Paradigm for Managing Change, Innovation, and Organizational Renewal* (San Francisco: Jossey-Bass, 1994).

Kindleberger, Charles P. *Manias, Panics, and Crashes: A History of Financial Crises* (NY: Wiley, 1996).

Komisar, Randy. *The Monk and the Riddle: The Education of a Silicon Valley Entrepreneur* (Boston, MA: Harvard Business School Press, 2000).

Kurzwell, Ray. *The Age of Spiritual Machines: When Computers Exceed Human Intelligence* (NY: Penguin Books, 1999).

Krugman, Paul. *The Return of Depression Economics* (1999); *The Accidental Theorist* (1998); *Pop Internationalism* (1996); and *Peddling Prosperity* (1994). All published by Norton.

Landes, David S. *The Wealth and Poverty of Nations: Why Some are So Rich and Some are So Poor* (NY: Norton, 1998).

Lawrence, Robert Z., Albert Bressand and Takatoshi Ito. *A Vision for the World Economy: Openness, Diversity, and Cohesion* (Washington, D.C.: Brookings Institution, 1996).

Leebaert, Derek, editor. *The Future of the Electronic Marketplace* (Cambridge, MA: MIT Press, 1998).

Levy, Frank. *The New Dollars and Dreams: American Incomes and Economic Change* (NY: Russell Sage Foundation, 1999).

Lewis, Michael. *The New New Thing* (NY: Norton, 2000).

Litan, Robert E. and William A. Niskanen. *Going Digital* (Washington, D.C.: Brookings, 1998).

Marshall, Ray and Marc Tucker. *Thinking for a Living: Education and the Wealth of Nations* (NY: Basic Books, 1992).

Micklethwait, John and Adrian Wooldridge. *The Witch Doctors: Making Sense of the Management Gurus* (NY: Times Business, 1997).

Mintzberg, Henry. *The Rise and Fall of Strategic Planning* (NY: Free Press, 1994).

Mokyr, Joel. *The Lever of Riches: Technological Creativity and Economic Progress*, Oxford University Press, 1990).

Moore, James F. *The Death of Competition: Leadership & Strategy in the Age of Business Ecosystems* (NY: HarperBusiness, 1996).

Moschella, David C. *Waves of Power: The Dynamics of Global Technology Leadership 1964–2010* (NY: AMACOM, 1997).

Neef, Dale, editor. *The Knowledge Economy* (Boston: Butterworth-Heinemann, 1998).

Negroponte, Nicholas. *Being Digital* (NY: Knopf, 1995).

Nocera, Joseph. *A Piece of the Action: How the Middle Class Joined the Money Class* (NY: Simon & Schuster, 1994).

Osborne, David and Ted Gaebler. *Reinventing Government* (Reading, MA: Addison-Wesley, 1992).

Osterman, Paul. *Securing Prosperity—The American Labor Market: How It Has Changed and What to Do about It* (Princeton University Press, 1999).

Peters, Thomas J. and Robert H. Waterman, Jr. *In Search of Excellence: Lessons from America's Best-Run Companies* (NY: Harper & Row, 1982).

Polanyi, Karl. *The Great Transformation: The Political and Economic Origins of Our Time* (Boston: Beacon Press, 1944).

Porter, E. Michael. *On Competition* (Boston: Harvard Business Review, 1998).

Postrel, Virginia. *The Future and its Enemies* (NY: Free Press, 1998).

Putnam, Robert D. *Bowling Alone: The Collapse and Revival of American Community* (NY: Simon & Schuster, 2000).

Raymond, Eric S. *The Cathedral & the Bazaar* (Sebastopol, CA: O'Reilly & Associates, 1999).

Reich, B. Robert. *The Work of Nations* (NY: Vintage, 1992).

Reid, Robert H. *Architects of the Web* (NY: Wiley, 1997).

Rodrik, Dani. *Has Globalization Gone Too Far?* (Washington, D.C.: Institute for International Economics, 1997).

Rogers, Everett M. *Diffusion of Innovations*, Fourth edition (NY: Free Press, 1995).

Rostow, W.W. *Theorists of Economic Growth from David Hume to the Present* (NY: Oxford University Press, 1990).

Saxenian, Annalee. *Regional Advantage: Culture and Competition in Silicon Valley and Route 128* (Cambridge, MA: Harvard University Press, 1998).

Schrage, Michael. *Serious Play: How the World's Best Companies Simulate to Innovate* (Boston: Harvard Business School Press, 2000).

Senge, Peter M., Charlotte Roberts, Richard B. Ross, Bryan J. Smith, and Art Kleiner. *The Fifth Discipline Fieldbook: Strategies and Tools for Building a Learning Organization* (NY: Doubleday, 1994).

Shapiro, Andrew L. *The Control Revolution: How the Internet is Putting Individuals in Charge and Changing the World We Know* (NY: PublicAffairs, 1999).

Shapiro, Carl and Hal R. Varian, *Information Rules: A Strategic Guide to the Network Economy* (Boston: Harvard Business School Press, 1999).

Sherraden, Michael, Lissa Johnson, Margaret Clancy, Sondra Beverly, Mark Schreiner, Min Zhan, and Jami Curley. *Saving Patterns in IDA Programs*, Center for Social Development, Washington University in St.Louis, January 2000.

Smith, Steven Rathgeb and Michael Lipsky. *Nonprofits for Hire: The Welfare State in the Age of Contracting* (Cambridge, MA: Harvard University Press, 1993).

Standage, Tom. *The Victorian Internet* (NY: Walker and Company, 1998).

Steurerle, C. Eugene, Edward M Gramlich, Hugh Heclo, and Demetra Smith Nightingale. *The Government We Deserve: responsive democracy and changing expectations* (Washington, D.C.: Urban Institute, 1998).

Stewart, Thomas A. *Intellectual Capital: The New Wealth of Organizations* (NY: Currency/Doubleday, 1997).

Stoll, Clifford. *Silicon Snake Oil: Second Thoughts on the Information Highway* (NY: Anchor/Doubleday, 1995).

Tapscott, Don, editor. *Creating Value in the Network Economy* (Boston: Harvard Business School Press, 1999).

Tapscott, Don. *The Digital Economy: Promise and Peril in the Age of Networked Intelligence* (NY: McGraw-Hill, 1996).

Thurow, Lester. *The Future of Capitalism: How Today's Economic Forces Shape Tomorrow's World* (NY: Morrow & Co., 1996).

Tzu, Sun. *The Art of War* (Boston: Shambhala, 1988).

U.S. Department of Housing and Urban Development, *The State of the Cities, 2000*, Fourth Annual, U.S. Department of Housing and Urban Development, Washington, D.C., June 2000.

Wilson, James Q. *Bureaucracy: What Government Agencies Do and Why They Do It* (NY: Basic Books, 1989).

Winston, Brian. *Media Technology and Society* (NY: Routledge, 1998).

RELATED WORK BY THE AUTHOR

Governance in the Digital Age: The Impact of the Global Economy, Information Technology, and Economic Regulation on State and Local Governments (Commissioned by seven national organizations serving state and local officials: CSG, ICMA, NACo, NCSL, NGA, NLC and USCM. Published in June 1999 by National League of Cities).

The State Role in Regulating Telecommunications—Municipal Right-of-Way and Franchise Fees (Commissioned and published by the Council of State Governments in October 1998.)

Is the New Global Economy Leaving State-Local Tax Structures Behind? (Commissioned by NGA, NCSL, and NLC. Published by the National League of Cities in 1998.)

TELEWARS in the States: Telecommunications Issues in a New Era of Competition (Published by the Council of Governors' Policy Advisors in June 1996; Distributed to the academic community by Lawrence Erlbaum Associates.)

"Is ISP-Bound Traffic 'Local' or 'Interstate'?, *Federal Communications Law Journal*, forthcoming.

State Strategies for the New Economy (Coauthor of multiple chapters.) Published by the National Governors' Association in February 2000; available from NGA's publication office: 301.498.3738; and www.nga.org/Pubs/IssueBriefs/2000/Strategies.asp.

"Taxing (and Not Taxing) Electronic Commerce," *State Tax Notes* (Vol. 17, no.18) November 1, 1999; shorter version in *Nation's Cities Weekly* (NLC), September 27, 1999 (See www.nlc.org/e-simp.htm); And, "**Retail E-commerce Threatens to Erode Public Sector Revenues**," *Nation's Cities Weekly*, November 29, 1999; (See www.gmanet.com/features/ecommerce/erode.shtml.)

The New State Role in Ensuring Universal Telecommunications Services, in *Making Universal Service Policy: Enhancing the Process Through Multidisciplinary Evaluation*, edited by Barbara Cherry, Alan Hammond, IV, and Steven Wildman, (1999) from Lawrence Erlbaum Associates: 201.236.9500.

How Scenarios Enrich Public Policy Decisions, (with Robert L. Olson) in *Learning from the Future: Competitive Foresight Scenarios*, edited by Liam Fahey & Robert M. Randall, published by John Wiley & Sons, 1998).

ABOUT THE AUTHOR

Tom Bonnett has had an extensive career in public policy, as a state legislator, a policy analyst, and as an advisor to public officials and nonprofit organizations. He was elected to the Vermont House of Representatives in 1974 and reelected in 1976. In Washington, D.C., he worked as a policy advisor for a member of Congress and for several nonprofit organizations. During the 1980s, he held several research positions in New York City government and served as Executive Director of the Downtown Flushing Development Corporation. During the 1990s, he worked for the Council of Governors' Policy Advisors, which published four of his books on a range of public policy topics, including *TELEWARS in the States* (1996).

Mr. Bonnett has become a frequent speaker at national and regional meetings of state and local officials, addressing state telecommunications issues, public finance challenges, and economic development strategies. Since becoming an independent policy consultant in 1997, his clients have included the Ford Foundation, National Academy of Public Administration, National Community Capital Association, and many national organizations serving state and local officials.

Tom Bonnett received a BA from Bennington College and an MPP from the University of California at Berkeley. He lives in Brooklyn, NY with a supportive wife and an eleven-year old son. His e-mail address is twbparkslo@aol.com.

Acknowledgments

I want to thank three sets of people. The first group includes people who have asked me to write about some of the topics addressed in this book. Theodore Roosevelt once wrote, "The best prize that life offers is the chance to work hard at work worth doing." Since becoming an independent consultant in 1997, I am extremely grateful to those who have given me opportunities to "to work hard at work worth doing." They include: Don Borut, National League of Cities; Gail Christopher, formerly at the National Academy of Public Administration; Tom Cochran, U. S. Conference of Mayors; Bill Hansell, International City/County Management Association; Larry Naake, National Association of County Officials; Chris Page, formerly of the Ford Foundation; Mark Pinsky, National Community Capital Association; Bill Pound, National Conference of State Legislatures; Ray Scheppach, National Governors' Association; Dan Sprague, Council of State Governments; and Costis Toregas, Public Technology, Inc.

The second group of people I want to thank are the hundreds of state and local government officials I have met in recent years. I have learned a great deal from these dedicated public servants. My conversations with people in the front lines of implementing information technologies and reinventing government were more valuable than anything yet published by the Harvard Business School Press (and it has great product). The public servants I have met are valiantly trying to improve government operations and public services. Their efforts are seldom appreciated by the public. I know I am not alone in my wish for a day when the honor of public service is restored to the level of respect it deserves.

The third group I want to thank is my loving and supportive family. They endured my frequent physical absences (when away on speaking trips) and mental absences (when lost in thought). Despite these frequent absences, they loved and encouraged me throughout this writing project. Thank you, Karen. Thank you, Stephen.